LOG CABINS
TODAY™

Edited By Jeanne Stauffer

HOUSE of
WHITE
BIRCHES

PUBLISHERS
SINCE 1947

LOG CABINS TODAY™

Editor **Jeanne Stauffer**
Art Director **Brad Snow**
Publishing Services Manager **Brenda Gallmeyer**

Editorial Assistant **Stephanie Franklin**
Assistant Art Director **Nick Pierce**
Copy Supervisor **Deborah Morgan**
Copy Editors **Emily Carter, Mary O'Donnell**
Technical Editor **Sandra L. Hatch**
Technical Proofreader **Angie Buckles**

Graphic Arts Supervisor **Erin Augsburger**
Graphic Artists **Glenda Chamberlain, Edith Teegarden**
Technical Artist **Connie Rand**
Production Assistants **Marj Morgan, Judy Neuenschwander**

Photography Supervisor **Tammy Christian**
Photography **Matthew Owen**
Photography Assistants **Tammy Liechty, Tammy Steiner**

Log Cabins Today is published by DRG, 306 East Parr Road, Berne, IN 46711.
Copyright © 2011 DRG. All rights reserved. This publication may not be reproduced
in part or in whole without written permission from the publisher.

Printed in China
Library of Congress Control Number: 2011920398
Hardcover ISBN: 978-1-59217-330-3
Softcover ISBN: 978-1-59217-331-0

RETAIL STORES: If you would like to carry this book or any other DRG publications,
visit DRGwholesale.com

Every effort has been made to ensure that the instructions in this publication
are complete and accurate. We cannot, however, take responsibility for human
error, typographical mistakes or variations in individual work. Please visit
ClotildeCustomerCare.com to check for pattern updates.

1 2 3 4 5 6 7 8 9 10

WELCOME

In a recent survey of quilters, over 75 percent named the Log Cabin block as their favorite traditional quilt block. There's a good reason for that. First, the Log Cabin block can be made using a wide variety of techniques. In this book, we give seven techniques for making Log Cabin blocks; each is illustrated with step-by-step photos. No matter how long you have been stitching Log Cabin quilts, you're sure to find at least one new method to try.

A second reason for the popularity of the Log Cabin block is its versatility. It can be used to frame other blocks or create a picture and can be any shape you want. You can make a quarter block, a half block or a block that is wonky, and the block is still recognizable by most quilters. All bear the familiar look of strips added around a central focal point. The versatility can also be seen in two variations of the Log Cabin block: the Courthouse Steps block and the Pineapple Log Cabin block. These blocks are almost as familiar as the traditional Log Cabin block itself.

A third reason for the popularity of the Log Cabin block is that it is so easy to piece that it is often the first quilt block that beginners make after they learn to piece two squares together. No matter if you are a beginner or an experienced quilter, this book has techniques for you to try—seven of them—and projects for you to make, a total of 32 designs by today's outstanding quilt designers.

From traditional to contemporary to modern to wonky, there are designs in this book for you. Have fun quilting and enjoy them all.

Warm regards,

Jeanne Stauffer

CONTENTS

LOG CABINS FOR BABY

LOG CABINS TO CELEBRATE

LOG CABINS TO VARY

Piecing With Strips

Cutting the strips used for a Log Cabin block and sewing them together by going around the center square is still the method that is used most often by quilters. We hope you will try all of the techniques presented in this book.

BY KAREN BLOCHER

BASIC INFORMATION

Select three fabrics for each half of the Log Cabin block and one for the center square. Fabrics may graduate in color from light to dark, dark to light or randomly.

For this illustration, I have chosen colors in neutral and blue batiks, but Log Cabin blocks look spectacular in fabrics of any color or style. Traditionally, the center square is often red or yellow to symbolize the hearth in your log cabin, but you may choose to use any color.

Once you have decided on a color scheme, it helps to draw a Log Cabin block and pin fabric samples to the "logs" to help you remember color placement.

Neutral thread colors such as taupe or gray are good choices for stitching blocks using fabrics with a variety of colors.

For ease of fabric handling and cutting, press all the fabrics you have chosen for your block using pressing spray, sizing or spray starch.

These instructions will result in an 8½"-square Log Cabin block, which, when joined with other blocks or borders, finishes at 8" square.

CUTTING

1. Cut one 2½" x 2½" center square. ***Note:*** *The sample uses the traditional red square in the center. Refer to Figure 1 for fabric numbers, with corresponding fabric colors, and their placement in the block.*

2. From fabric 1 (lightest neutral in this sample) cut one each 1½" x 2½" and 1½" x 3½" rectangle.

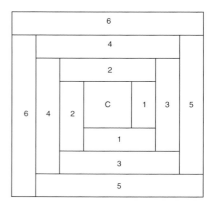

Figure 1

Fabric Key for Log Cabin Block

Center—red
Fabric 1—lightest neutral
Fabric 2—lightest blue
Fabric 3—medium neutral
Fabric 4—medium blue
Fabric 5—darkest neutral
Fabric 6—darkest blue

3. From fabric 2 (lightest blue in this sample) cut one each 1½" x 3½" and 1½" x 4½" rectangle.

4. From fabric 3 (medium neutral in this sample) cut one each 1½" x 4½" and 1½" x 5½" rectangle.

5. From fabric 4 (medium blue in this sample) cut one each 1½" x 5½" and 1½" x 6½" rectangle.

6. From fabric 5 (darkest neutral in this sample) cut one each 1½" x 6½" and 1½" x 7½" rectangle.

7. From fabric 6 (darkest blue in this sample) cut one each 1½" x 7½" and 1½" x 8½" rectangle.

PIECING THE BLOCK

Note: *Use ¼" seams throughout.*

1. Begin by stitching the 1½" x 2½" fabric 1 rectangle to the right side of the center square; press seam allowance toward the rectangle (photo 1).

2. Measure the unit; it should be 2½" x 3½". Trim the unit to this size, if necessary.

3. Stitch the 1½" fabric 1 rectangle to the bottom edge of the pieced unit; press seam toward the rectangle (photo 2).

4. Measure stitched unit—it should be 3½" x 3½". Trim the unit to this size, if necessary.

5. Working clockwise, add the 1½" x 3½" fabric 2 rectangle to the left side of the pieced unit to make a 3½" x 4½" unit; press and check size (photo 3). Repeat with the 1½" x 4½" fabric 2 rectangle, add it to the top of the block to make a 4½" x 4½" square unit; press and check size (photo 4).

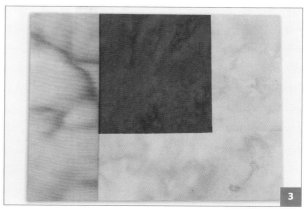

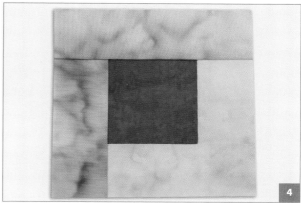

6. Still working clockwise, add the 1½" x 4½" fabric 3 rectangle to the first fabric 1 rectangle side of the pieced unit and the 1½" x 5½" fabric 3 rectangle to the second fabric 1 rectangle side of the pieced unit to make a 5½" x 5½" square (photo 5). Press seams toward rectangles and check size.

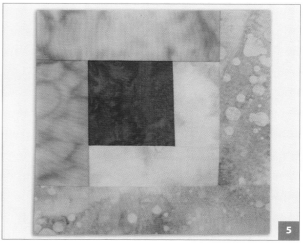

7. Still working clockwise, add the 1½" x 5½" fabric 4 rectangle to the first fabric 2 rectangle side of the pieced unit and the 1½" x 6½" fabric 4 rectangle to the second fabric 2 rectangle side of the pieced unit to make a 6½" x 6½" square (photo 6). Press seams toward rectangles and check size.

8. Still working clockwise, add the 1½" x 6½" fabric 5 rectangle to the first fabric 3 rectangle side of the pieced unit and the 1½" x 7½" fabric 5 rectangle to the second fabric 3 rectangle side of the pieced unit to make a 7½" x 7½" square (photo 7). Press seams toward rectangles and check size.

9. Still working clockwise, add the 1½" x 7½" fabric 6 rectangle to the first fabric 4 rectangle side of the pieced unit and the 1½" x 8½" fabric 6 rectangle to

the second fabric 4 rectangle side of the pieced unit to make an 8½" x 8½" square (photo 8). Press seams toward rectangles and check size to finish one Log Cabin block. ■

Mistake to Avoid

It is easy to make a mistake and place a rectangle on the wrong side of a block (compare this photo to photo 5). This will interrupt the pattern. If you turn your pieced unit so that the most recently added strip is closest to you when placed under the presser foot, then the strip you want to add should be placed on top of the pieced unit on the side under the presser foot. Keeping the most recently added strip facing you every time guarantees that you will be adding the next strip to the correct side of the pieced unit.

CRACK IN THE WALL

Log Cabin blocks create the stone wall with cracks that host the morning glory flowers and vines. Use traditional piecing of strips to create the blocks and permanent fabric pens or colored pencils to add the vines and flower details.

DESIGN BY BRENDABARB DESIGNS, BRENDA CONNELLY & BARBARA MILLER

PROJECT NOTES

Refer to Piecing on page 6 for detailed photo step-by-step instructions for Piecing the Log Cabin blocks for this wall quilt.

PROJECT SPECIFICATIONS

Skill Level: Intermediate
Quilt Size: 33½" x 33½"
Block Size: 12" x 12"
Number of Blocks: 4

MATERIALS

- 3½" x 12" pink batik for pink morning glory
- 3½" x 9" lavender batik for lavender morning glory
- ⅛ yard medium green batik or 2 or 3 rectangles 3" x 12" different greens for leaves
- ⅛ yard dark green mottled
- ¼ yard each 4–7 cream/light green batiks for Log Cabin strips
- ¼ yard each 3–6 medium green batiks for Log Cabin strips
- ¼ yard dark green batik
- ⅞ yard light blue batik
- Batting 41" x 41"
- Backing 41" x 41"
- All-purpose thread to match fabrics
- Quilting thread
- Black and green permanent fabric pens or machine-embroidery threads
- ½ yard 18"-wide fusible web

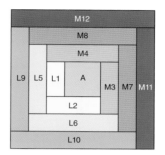

Log Cabin
12" x 12" Block
Make 4

- Appliqué pressing sheet (optional)
- Colored pencils, oil pastels and/or opaque fabric paints for detailing flowers and leaves
- Chalk pencil
- Basic sewing tools and supplies

CUTTING

1. Starting with the lightest fabric, cut the following from the 4–7 assorted lights:

4–2" x 3½" L1
4–2" x 5" L2
4–2" x 6½" L5
4–2" x 8" L6
4–2" x 9½" L9
4–2" x 11" L10
2–2" x 12½" B
1–2" x 25½" C

2. Starting with the lightest fabric, cut the following from the 3–6 assorted mediums:

4–2" x 5" M3
4–2" x 6½" M4
4–2" x 8" M7
4–2" 9½" M8
4–2" x 11" M11
4–2" x 12½" M12

3. Cut one 4½" x 10" rectangle dark green batik; set aside for leaves.

4. Cut two 1" x 26" D strips and 1" x 27" E strips from the remaining dark green batik fabric.

5. Cut four 4" by fabric with strips light blue batik. Subcut strips into two 27" F strips, two 34" G strips and four 3½" x 3½" A squares.

6. Cut four 2¼" by fabric width strips light blue batik for binding.

7. Set aside remainder of fabrics for appliqué.

COMPLETING THE BLOCKS

1. Select one strip of each size and one A square for one Log Cabin block.

2. Sew the L1 strip to the A square as shown in Figure 1; press seam toward the strip.

Figure 1

3. Continue adding strips in numerical order with L strips on one side and M strips on the other side of the center square, referring to Figure 2 to complete one Log Cabin block.

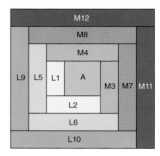

Figure 2

4. Repeat steps 1–3 to complete a total of four Log Cabin squares.

COMPLETING THE TOP

1. Join two Log Cabin blocks with a B strip to make a row as shown in Figure 3; press seams toward B strips. Repeat to make two rows.

Figure 3

2. Join the two rows with the C strip to complete the pieced center as shown in Figure 4; press seams toward C strip.

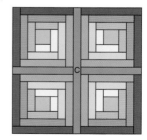

Figure 4

3. Sew D strips to the top and bottom and E strips to opposite sides of the pieced center; press seams toward D and E strips.

4. Sew F strips to the top and bottom and G strips to opposite sides of the pieced center; press seams toward F and G strips to complete the pieced top.

COMPLETING THE APPLIQUÉ

1. Trace individual appliqué shapes onto the paper side of the fusible web as directed on each piece for number to cut; cut out shapes, leaving a margin around each one. ***Note:*** *You may choose to vary the blossoms and leaves by turning the pattern upside down before tracing some of the pieces and/or turning blossoms in different directions. The patterns are already reversed for fusible appliqué.*

2. Fuse paper shapes to the wrong side of fabrics as directed on each piece for color; cut out shapes on the traced lines.

Crack in the Wall
Placement Diagram 33½" x 33½"

3. Place the pieces fabric side up over the appliqué motif sample pattern on a light box or window and trace in details using a permanent fabric pen.

4. Using a chalk pencil, lightly draw vines and stems onto the pieced top beginning in the corner on one outer border and continuing design onto an additional border, referring to the Placement Diagram and project photos for positioning suggestions. ***Note:*** *Some of the vines come out of the logs, thus inspiring the project name Crack in the Wall.*

5. Using the black permanent fabric pen, outline the vines and stems. Fill in with green permanent fabric pen.

6. Arrange the leaves and flowers in place on the vines and stems. When satisfied with placement of pieces, fuse in place.

7. Add vines and stems, and then appliqué pieces to the Log Cabin blocks as in steps 4–6.

8. When all pieces have been fused in place, machine-stitch pieces in place using a narrow, close blanket stitch and thread to match fabrics.

Completing the Quilt

1. Layer, quilt and bind referring to Finishing Your Quilt on page 175. ■

Optional Painting

Shading and details may be added to flowers and leaves using colored pencils, oil pastels and/or fabric paint. This should be done before individual pieces are cut from fabrics as follows:

• Add highlights to leaves using yellow.
• Add white in the centers of flowers.
• Add darker colors of pink and purple to define petals.
• Lay the pieces fabric side up on an ironing board and place an appliqué pressing sheet on top; iron pieces to help set colors. Let cool.
• Cut out shapes on traced lines and remove paper backing.

Bud Base
Cut 4 medium
green scrap

Morning Glory 2
Cut 2 each lavender & pink batiks

Morning Glory 1
Cut 1 lavender & 2 pink batiks

Bud
Cut 2 each lavender
& pink batiks

Leaf 3
Cut 3 medium green batik

Leaf 4
Cut 1 medium green batik
& 3 dark green mottled

Leaf 1
Cut 1 each dark green mottled
& dark green batik &
3 medium green scrap

Leaf 2
Cut 3 medium
green batik or
scraps & 2 dark
green mottled

Appliqué Motif Sample
This sample shows 1 layout possibility using flower and leaf patterns
provided. Stems, flower and leaf details have been added.

Paper Piecing

Paper piecing is one of the most accurate ways to make a Log Cabin block. The traditional method of placing the fabric on the block and turning the block over to do the stitching is easy enough for a beginner.

BY CONNIE KAUFFMAN

PAPER PIECING

Making paper-pieced quilt blocks is a great way to make very accurate blocks. Fabrics are sewn to a paper foundation with a close stitch length. One of the benefits of paper piecing is that the fabrics do not have to be cut to the precise size. The paper pattern remains on the blocks until the top is finished for added stability. Once the paper is removed and the top is pressed, you are ready for quilting!

MAKING THE PATTERNS

1. Count the blocks needed for your design and make a photocopy pattern for each block. Regular computer paper may be used, but thinner papers are easier to remove. There are several choices in papers, as well as a water-soluble paper that can be used. Check out the choices at your local quilt shop or online.

2. After printing your initial pattern, double-check to make sure it is the same size as the original pattern. Some copiers may cause slight distortion, so be sure to double-check before making all of your copies.

3. Cut out the patterns along the outside bold lines. On the marked side of each pattern, write what color goes in which space. (*Remember that all patterns are reversed on the paper copies.*) You can also shade areas that will be the same color—in our sample, all the black strips are shaded gray.

SEWING THE BLOCKS

1. Look at the paper pattern and measure the size of the center block marked 1. Add ¼" to each side (or ½" total), and cut the center fabric piece that size or slightly larger. ***Note:*** *The exact measurement is not important as you will be trimming excess fabric in each step. Having a bit more fabric allows for slight movements in fabric placement.*

Saving Time

Most Log Cabin patterns use the same color/fabric for the center square. In the sample shown, the center is blue. To speed up your quilting time, it is helpful to cut all the centers the correct size and set those aside until you start another block. This eliminates measuring the centers again for each block.

2. Place the fabric right side up on the opposite side of the printed block over the space marked for piece 1. It is often helpful to hold the block up to the light to make sure you have completely covered the space with fabric extending around each side. For this first block, it is helpful to place a small spot of water-soluble glue on the paper to hold the first fabric piece until the second fabric is sewn (photo 1).

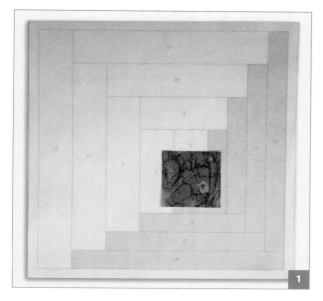

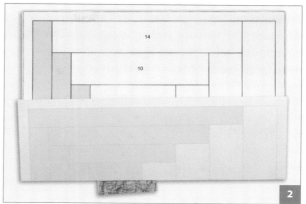

3. Turn the block over and fold the paper toward you along each outside line of the block. Trim any excess fabric that extends ¼" beyond each folded side. Trim with scissors or lay the block on a cutting mat and trim with a ruler and rotary cutter. Exact cutting is not required (photo 2).

4. Measure the size of piece 2 and add ¼" to each side; cut a colored fabric scrap that size or slightly larger—if you have precut the fabric strips, you will no longer have to measure and cut.

5. Place piece 2 right side down on top of the first fabric. One edge of piece 2 should be even with the stitched edge of piece 1.

6. Set your machine to a very close stitch (18–20 stitches per inch) so that later, the paper will tear away from the sewing line easier.

Precut the Strips

Look at your Log Cabin block to see what colors are used in the surrounding strips and if any are the same width. If strips are the same width, you can precut the strips and have them ready to use. Using strips in the approximate correct size is easier than trying to hold large pieces of fabric when sewing.

In the sample, all of the black strips, or logs, are the same width (½"), so strips of black fabric could be cut 1" wide and set aside, ready to use (the log is ½", adding ¼" to each side for seam allowances makes the strips cut 1" wide). The length of the strip is not important as you will cut and sew as you go along. The wider logs are all cut from scrap fabrics. These logs are ⅞" wide, finished, so you can cut your colored scrap strips 1½" (⅞" finished width, plus ¼" to each side equal 1⅜", but 1½" is an easier size to cut, and in this technique, that extra ⅛" doesn't matter).

7. Hold or pin the pieces together; turn over and sew along the line between pieces 1 and 2. Begin sewing ¼" from the line and end ¼" past the line—there is no need to backstitch (photos 3 and 4).

paper along each side of piece 2; trim excess fabric to ¼" on each side. Where seams have been sewn through the line, carefully tear the paper from the seam so you are able to fold back the paper (photo 5).

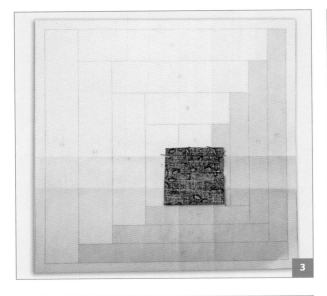

9. Select piece 3 according to the pattern (black in the sample). Lay it right side down on top of pieces 1 and 2 with one edge of the piece even with the edges of pieces 1 and 2 that overlap piece 3 stitching line.

10. Turn the pattern over and sew on the line between pieces 1, 2 and 3. Flip the fabric back, press and trim as in step 8. ***Note:*** *Always look to see what number and color strip is next to sew. Continue adding strips in the same manner until all strips have been added.*

Ripping Seams

If you have to rip out a seam and the paper tears, simply place clear tape over the seam line and sew over the tape.

8. Trim excess fabric from the seam. Fold piece 2 to the right side and press flat. Pin or use a small dab of glue stick to help hold piece 2 in place. As with piece 1, turn the pattern with the lines facing up and finger-press the

11. After you have sewn strip 4, the next strip to be sewn will always be the one that has three fabrics to sew over. It will have two sewn seams to sew over. Piece 5 will be placed on top of pieces 1, 2 and 4 (photo 6). Continue to sew all strips in this same manner.

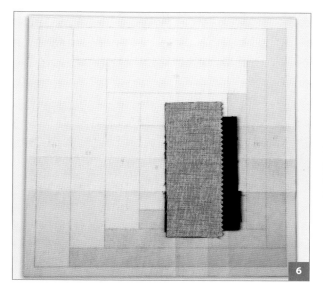

12. When all the pieces have been stitched and pressed, trim excess fabric from all of the outside edges along marked lines on the paper pattern. Do not remove paper (photos 7 and 8)

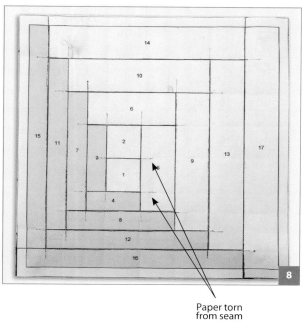

Paper torn from seam

JOINING THE BLOCKS

1. Lay the blocks out in rows; pin together, matching edges.

2. Sew along the marked ¼" seam line.

3. Tear off the ¼" paper along the seam edges and press seams in one direction.

4. Join the rows in the same manner and remove the ¼" paper along the seam edges after seams are sewn.

5. After the blocks are all sewn together, remove the remainder of the paper by pressing your fingernail against the sewn line and tearing gently. ■

RADIANT STAR

Use traditional paper piecing to stitch this striking throw. Narrow strips of black for half of the block give it a contemporary look.

DESIGN BY CONNIE KAUFFMAN

PROJECT NOTES

Refer to Paper Piecing on page 14 for detailed photo step-by-step instructions for paper piecing.

PROJECT SPECIFICATIONS

Skill Level: Advanced Beginner
Quilt Size: 50½" x 50½"
Block Size: 6¼" x 6¼"
Number of Blocks: 36

MATERIALS

- Scraps assorted light- and medium-color fabrics for log strips
- ⅛ yard bright blue print
- 2½ yards black solid
- Batting 58" x 58"
- Backing 58" x 58"
- Neutral-color all-purpose thread
- Quilting thread
- Basic sewing tools and supplies

CUTTING

1. Cut two 1½" by fabric width strips bright blue print; subcut strips into (36) 1½" A squares.

2. Cut one 7" by fabric width strip black solid; subcut strip into four 7" D squares.

3. Cut eight 3¼" x 38" B strips black solid.

4. Cut six 21/4" by fabric width strips black solid for binding.

5. Cut (30) 1" by fabric width strips black solid for black log strips.

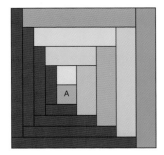

Uneven Log Cabin
6¼" x 6¼" Block
Make 20

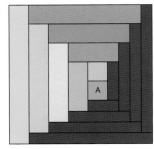

Reversed Uneven Log Cabin
6¼" x 6¼" Block
Make 16

6. Cut the assorted light- and medium-color scraps into 1½"-wide strips for colored log strips.

COMPLETING THE BLOCKS

1. Place the A square right side up on the unprinted side of a paper-piecing pattern over the space marked for piece 1 as shown in Figure 1. ***Note:*** *It is often helpful to hold the block up to the light to make sure you have completely covered the space with fabric extending around each side. For this first block, it is helpful to place a small spot of water-soluble glue on the paper to hold the first fabric piece until the second fabric is sewn.*

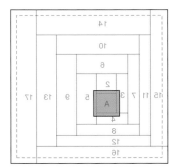

Figure 1

2. Measure the size of piece 2 and add ¼" to each side; cut a colored fabric piece that size or slightly larger from the 1½"-wide scrap strips.

3. Place piece 2 right side down on A—the edge of piece 2 should be even with the edge of A.

4. Set your machine to a very close stitch—18–20 stitches per inch.

5. Hold or pin the pieces together; turn over and sew on the paper side along the line between pieces A and 2. Begin sewing ¼" from the line and end ¼" past the line as shown in Figure 2.

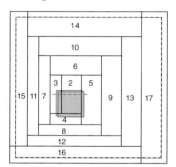

Figure 2

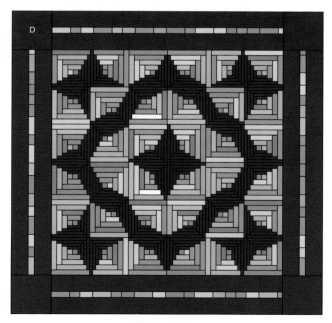

Radiant Star
Placement Diagram 50½" x 50½"

6. Fold piece 2 to the right side and finger-press flat. Pin or use a small dab of glue stick to help hold piece 2 in place.

7. Continue to cut pieces as in step 2, cutting narrow pieces from black log strips and wider pieces from colored log strips.

8. Add the pieces around A until the paper is covered.

9. When all the pieces have been stitched and pressed, trim excess fabric from all of the outside edges along marked lines on the paper pattern. Do not remove paper.

10. Repeat steps 1–9 to complete a total of 20 Uneven Log Cabin blocks and 16 Reversed Uneven Log Cabin blocks.

JOINING THE BLOCKS

1. Select three each Uneven Log Cabin and Reversed Uneven Log Cabin blocks.

2. Arrange and join the blocks along the marked seam edge of paper patterns to make an X row as shown in Figure 3; press seams in one direction. Repeat to make a second X row.

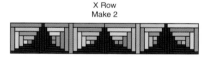

X Row
Make 2

Figure 3

3. Tear off the ¼" paper along the seam edges and press seams in one direction.

4. Repeat Steps 1–3 to make two Y rows referring to Figure 4.

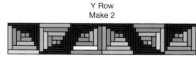

Y Row
Make 2

Figure 4

5. Select four Uneven Log Cabin and two Reversed Uneven Log Cabin blocks.

6. Repeat steps 2 and 3 to make two Z rows referring to Figure 5.

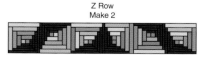

Z Row
Make 2

Figure 5

7. Arrange and join the X, Y and Z rows to complete the pieced center referring to Figure 6; press seams in one direction.

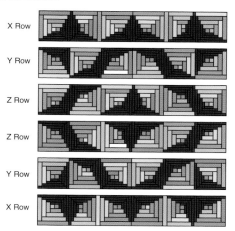

Figure 6

8. After the blocks are all sewn together, remove the remainder of the paper by pressing your fingernail against the sewn line and tearing gently.

COMPLETING THE QUILT

1. Select some of the remaining 1½"-wide colored log strips and join on short ends to make four 38" C strips; press seams in one direction.

2. Sew a C strip between two B strips along length to make a B-C strip as shown in Figure 7; press seams toward B strips. Repeat to make a total of four B-C strips.

Figure 7

3. Sew a B-C strip to opposite sides of the pieced center; press seams toward B-C strips.

4. Sew a D square to each end of each remaining B-C strip; press seams away from C.

5. Sew a B-C-D strip to the top and bottom of the pieced center to complete the quilt top; press seams toward B-C-D strips.

6. Layer, quilt and bind referring to Finishing Your Quilt on page 175. ■

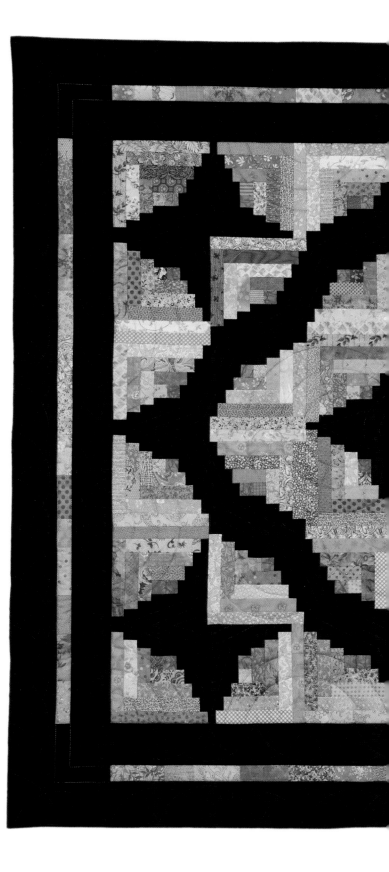

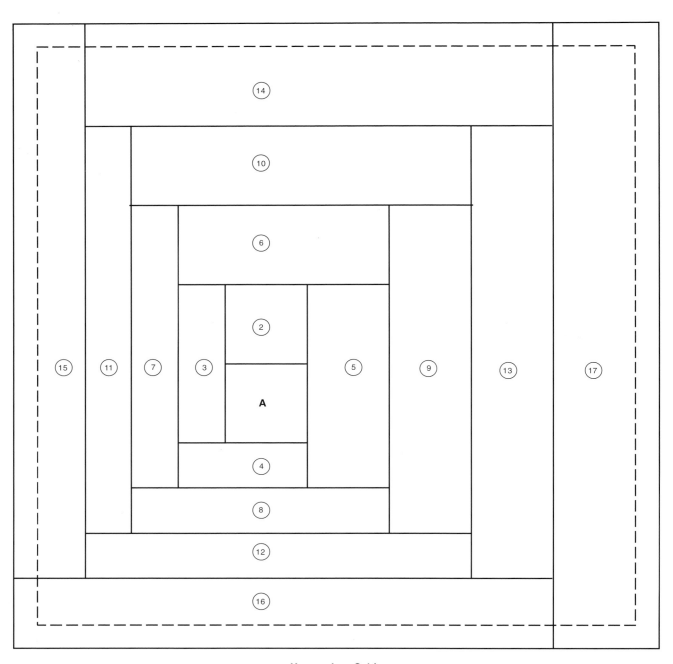

Uneven Log Cabin
Paper-Piecing Pattern
Make 20 copies

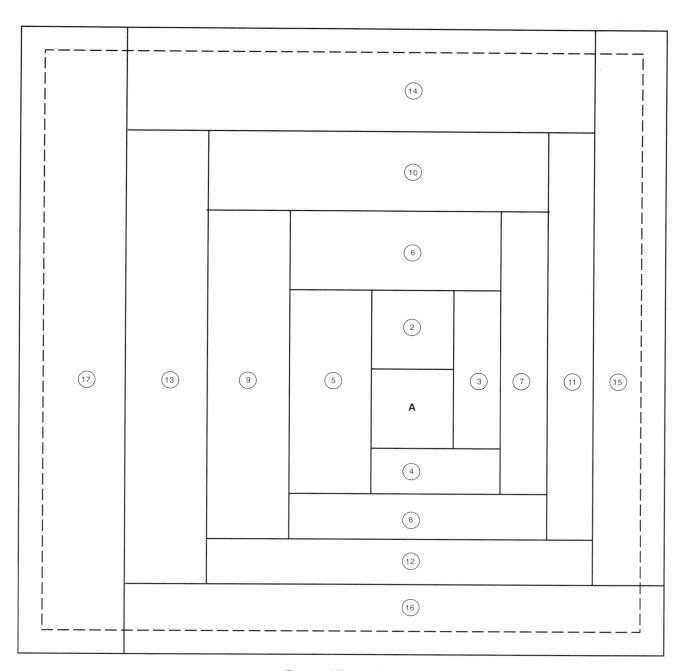

Reversed Uneven Log Cabin
Paper-Piecing Pattern
Make 16 copies

Free-Form Foundation Piecing

This technique was used for many antique Log Cabin quilts; it makes it easier to use small scraps of fabric.

BY JULIE HIGGINS

USING FABRIC FOUNDATIONS

Pre-printed muslin foundations are available in a variety of patterns and sizes. You can also trace foundations, print them from the computer onto fabric and even use rubber stamps made just for marking foundation patterns on fabric. For these types of foundation piecing, see instructions for paper piecing because the technique will be exactly the same, except there is *no* need to decrease the stitch length as there is *no* paper to remove. The fabric foundation remains in the finished quilt.

The following technique is fast, easy, fun and forgiving. There are few rulers. You are not sewing on a pre-printed line, and so all sewing is done from the front of the block. You are not precutting exact strips, so get out your scraps and give it a try.

There are two ways to make a Log Cabin block with this method—you may begin with a square on one corner or with a square in the center of the foundation square.

FOUNDATION PIECING ON MUSLIN

1. Cut a 9" x 9" square muslin. **Note:** *Always cut the muslin foundation at least ½" larger than needed. You will cut off the extra when you trim the block.*

2. Cut a square of fabric to use as a starting point—2"–3" is a good size to start with. It doesn't have to be exact, and it doesn't have to be straight.

3. Pin the square on the muslin foundation right side up—you can start in a corner to make a quarter-Log

Cabin block (Block A/photo 1) like the blocks in La Luz Del Sol on page 27 or start in the center as in a traditional Log Cabin block (Block B/photo 2).

Block A

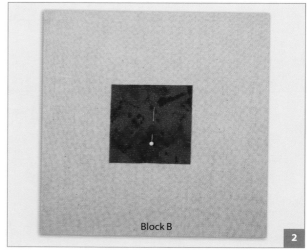

Block B

4. Cut a strip of fabric at least as long as the square that was pinned to the foundation square—this is one of the few rules. It can be longer and then trimmed after stitching, but it can't be shorter. It can be anywhere from 1"–3" wide.

5. Place this strip right side down on the starting square and sew through all layers—strip, square and muslin (photos 3 and 4).

Block A

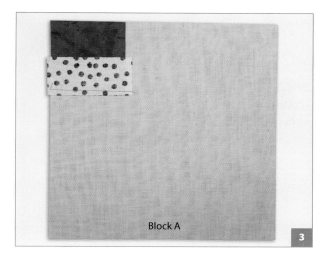

Block A

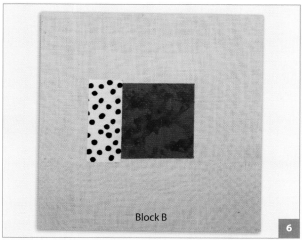

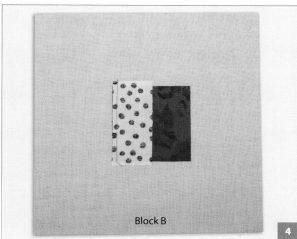

Block B

6. Flip the strip to the right side and press flat (photos 5 and 6).

Block B

7. Sew another strip to the next side (photo 7) or the other side for quarter-Log Cabin block (photo 8),

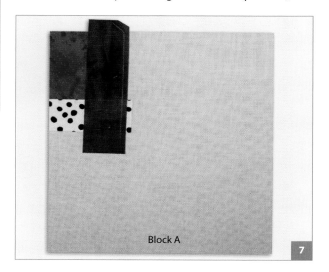

Block A

making sure the strip is at least as long as the side you are covering—at this point this will include the starting square plus one strip. You don't need to measure—just grab a strip or scrap and hold it against the next seam line to be sure it is long enough. Flip this strip to the right side and press flat

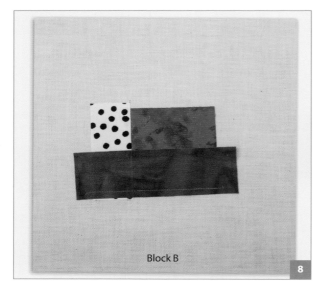

Block B

8. Continue to add strips either on opposite sides or round and round until you have covered the foundation square (photos 9 and 10).

Block A

Block B

9. Press the stitched unit.

10. Trim the covered foundation square to 8½" x 8½" to complete the block—it will measure 8" x 8" when stitched together with other blocks using a ¼" seam allowance. ■

Free-form Foundation Piecing Ideas

Free-form foundation piecing is perfect for use in the quilt-as-you-go method. To do this, layer each foundation square with a same-size batting and backing square, and use a quilting foot or walking foot as you sew pieces to the foundation square. The thread will show on the backing square, so choose thread for the bobbin that will blend in with the square.

Other ideas include starting the piecing with a triangle and going around three sides until the foundation is covered. Or, make a crazy quilt using any shape. Start with an odd shape or a specific motif in the center of the foundation square and build around it to finish the blocks.

Experiment with wide and narrow strips, scraps, novelty prints and shapes of any size or shape. Have fun making free-form Log Cabin blocks.

LA LUZ DEL SOL

The traditional Log Cabin quilt has a red or yellow square in the center. This foundation-pieced quilt uses quarter-Log Cabin blocks that look like the light of the sun is shining through an open window or doorway.

DESIGN BY JULIE HIGGINS

PROJECT NOTES

This project is a free-form quarter-Log Cabin block made on a muslin foundation. It's a fun and easy quilt to make with lots of layout possibilities. In this layout, it looks like the light of the sun is coming through a doorway at the top of the stairs leading up.

Because it is sewn on a permanent foundation, this quilt will hold up well with embellishments, such as beads.

PROJECT SPECIFICATIONS

Skill Level: Beginner
Quilt Size: 58" x 34"
Block Size: 8" x 8"
Number of Blocks: 18

MATERIALS

- Scraps or ⅛–¼-yard cuts of at least 15 fabrics, some with reds/oranges/yellow for A
- ⅝ yard black solid
- ⅞ yard black-with-white swirls
- 1⅜ yards muslin
- Batting 66" x 42"
- Backing 66" x 42'
- Neutral-color all-purpose thread
- Quilting thread
- Basic sewing tools and supplies

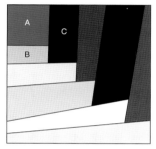

La Luz Del Sol
8" x 8" Block
Make 18

CUTTING

1. Cut five 9" by fabric width strips muslin; subcut strips into (18) 9" foundation squares.

2. Cut (18) 2"–4" A squares/rectangles in a mixture of red, orange and yellow.

3. Free-form cut a variety of strips 1"–3" wide in a variety of lengths from 3"–9" from the 15 fabrics or scraps, half light for B and half dark for C.

4. Cut two 3½" x 24½" D strips black solid.

5. Cut three 3½" by fabric width strips black solid. Join strips on short ends to make one long strip; press seams open. Subcut strip into two 54½" E strips.

6. Cut two 2½" x 30½" F strips black-with-white swirls.

7. Cut three 2½" by fabric width strips black-with-white swirls. Join strips on short ends to make one long strip; press seams open. Subcut strip into two 58½" G strips.

8. Cut five 2¼" by fabric width binding strips black-with-white swirls.

COMPLETING THE BLOCKS

1. Select one muslin foundation square, one A piece and one B strip at least as long as the A square. Pin the A piece right side up on one corner of the foundation square as shown in Figure 1.

Figure 1

2. Place the B strip right side down on the right edge of A, starting one end at the edge of the foundation and letting the other end extend beyond A as shown in Figure 2; sew ¼" through all layers, stopping stitching at the end of A as shown in Figure 3.

Figure 2

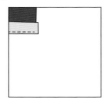

Figure 3

3. Flip the B strip to the right side and press flat as shown in Figure 4.

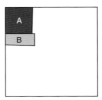

Figure 4

4. Select a C strip at least as long as A and B combined and repeat step 2; trim the excess B even with the edge of C, and flip C to the right side and press flat as shown in Figure 5.

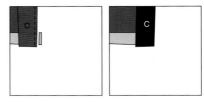

Figure 5

5. Continue adding B and C strips as in steps 2–4 until the muslin foundation square is completely covered. *Note: The strips may extend beyond the edges of the muslin square at this time.*

6. Trim the stitched foundation block to 8½" x 8½" to finish.

7. Repeat steps 1–6 to complete a total of 18 blocks.

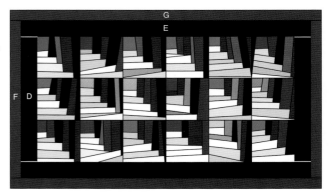

La Luz Del Sol
Placement Diagram 58" x 34"

COMPLETING THE QUILT

1. Select six blocks and join with the A squares oriented in the same orientation to make a row as shown in Figure 6; press seams in one direction. Repeat to make three rows.

Figure 6

2. Join the rows, referring to the Placement Diagram for positioning; press seams in one direction.

3. Sew a D strip to the short ends and E strips to the long sides of the pieced center; press seams toward D and E strips.

4. Sew an F strip to the short ends and G strips to the long sides of the pieced center; press seams toward the F and G strips to complete the pieced top.

5. Layer, quilt and bind referring to Finishing Your Quilt on page 175. ■

Quilt As You Go

Quilting as you go is great for those who would rather piece strips than quilt. When you add the last strip, the quilt is finished. How easy is that!

BY CAROL ZENTGRAF

Create reversible blocks that are quilted as you piece them when you use this time-saving technique. It is ideal for making quilts of any size and is especially ideal for larger quilts that you would have difficulty quilting on a standard sewing machine.

The basic quilt-as-you-go technique refers to a stitch-and-flip process where strips are stitched to a batting-topped backing square or to the assembly of completed blocks into a quilt. A variation of this is used to create a block that features the Log Cabin piecing on both the block front and the backing.

Identical strips are cut for the block fabric, batting and backing fabrics and all three strips are added simultaneously. It is ideal for traditional Log Cabin piecing with straight strips or for creating an unstructured block as shown in the Crazy Blocks Quilt on page 32.

Refer to the following instructions to make a quilt-as-you-go unstructured block using this quilt-as-you-go variation.

QUILT-AS-YOU-GO

1. Select a mixture of five to 10 print and solid fabrics for the quilt top. **Note:** *You can use the same fabric for the backing strips or a variety of fabrics as for the top. The yardage needed will depend on the size of your quilt. Use needled cotton batting or other low-loft batting.*

2. From each fabric, cut a variety of strips across the width of the fabric in widths ranging from 1"–3". Repeat to cut batting strips in the same widths.

3. To begin, cut an identical center square or rectangle each from the top fabric, batting and backing. Layer the backing fabric right side down, batting and top fabric right side up.

4. To add the first set of strips to the center, select a strip width and cut one strip each from a top fabric strip, batting strip and backing fabric strip a little longer than one side of the center square. **Note:** *It isn't necessary to measure the length of the strips as long as they are slightly longer than the edge you will be sewing them to.*

5. Place the top strip along one edge of the center square top fabric with right sides together. Repeat to place the backing strip along the same edge of the backing fabric.

6. Place the batting strip on the wrong side of the top strip. Stitch the layers together using a ¼" seam allowance. Trim the batting close to the stitching (photo 1).

7. Open the strips right sides out and press the seam allowance away from the center (photo 2). Trim the short ends even with the center; trim the long edges even, if necessary.

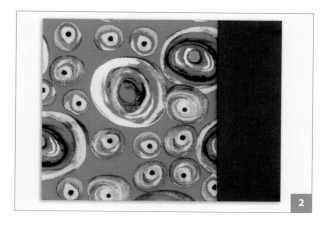

8. Repeat step 4 to cut a set of strips slightly longer than one combined edge of the center block and first set of strips.

9. Sandwich the edge between the top and backing strips with right sides together and the batting strip on the wrong side of the top strip. Stitch the edges together; trim the batting close to the stitching (photo 3).

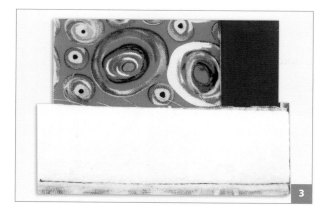

10. Press the strips away from the center and trim the ends (photo 4).

11. Continue adding strips around the block, alternating widths and fabrics as desired. To create an unstructured look, cut the long edges of random strips at an angle after stitching them to the block (photo 5).

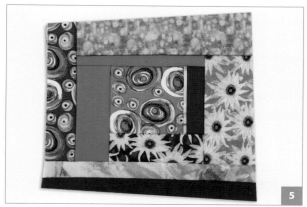

12. Piece strips around the block until it is slightly larger than the desired finished size. Trim edges and square corners as needed to complete the block (photo 6). ◼

CRAZY BLOCKS QUILT

This quilt uses the quilt-as-you-go method with strips of all different sizes and shapes, so no two blocks are the same. Some of the strips are leftovers from projects and are already pieced together, creating a truly scrappy quilt.

DESIGN BY CAROL ZENTGRAF

PROJECT NOTE

Refer to Quilt-As-You-Go Log Cabin Technique instructions and step-by-step photos, on page 30, as you complete the blocks and sashing of this Crazy Block Quilt.

PROJECT SPECIFICATIONS

Skill Level: Advanced
Quilt Size: 64" x 80"
Block Size: Approximately 14"–15" x 16"–18"
Number of Blocks: 16

MATERIALS

- Assorted print and solid fabrics to total 10 yards for blocks, sashing and binding
- 3 yards 90"-wide cotton batting
- Neutral-color all-purpose thread
- Quilting thread
- Basic sewing tools and supplies

CUTTING

1. Cut (32) 4" x 4" A squares from assorted prints and solids. **Note:** *Sixteen of the squares are for the block back center.* Cut (16) 4" x 4" batting squares.

2. Set aside 3"–5"-wide strips for B and C sashing strips.

3. Cut and piece 2¼"-wide strips for binding to total 290".

4. Cut all remaining fabrics for front and back blocks into 1½"–3½"-wide strips.

5. Cut batting strips to match the width sizes of each block strip.

Crazy Blocks
14"–15" x 16"–18"
Make 16

COMPLETING THE BLOCKS

1. Layer the backing A square right side down, batting and front-side A square right side up; pin to hold. **Note:** *Layers of three pieces (backing, batting and front) are referred to as a set in the instructions that follow.*

2. To add the first set of strips to the center A set, select one same-size front strip, back strip and batting strip a little longer than one side of the center square. **Note:** *It isn't necessary to measure the length of the strips as long as they are slightly longer than the edge you will be sewing them to.*

3. Place the front-side strip along one edge of the front side of the A set with right sides together. Place the backing strip along the same edge of the back of the A set.

4. Place the batting strip on the top side of the front-side strip. Stitch the layers together using a ¼" seam

allowance as shown in Figure 1. Trim the batting close to the stitching referring to Figure 2. **Note**: *If you find stitching ¼" seams with all the layers to be difficult, try using a ½" seam allowance and trim to ¼" after stitching.*

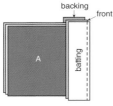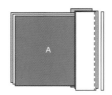

Figure 1   **Figure 2**

5. Open the strips right sides out and press the seam allowance away from A. Trim the short ends even with the A set as shown in Figure 3. Cut the strips at a random angle, again referring to Figure 3.

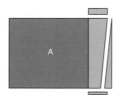

Figure 3

6. Repeat step 2 to cut a same-width set of front, backing and batting strips slightly longer than the combined edge of A and first set of added strips.

7. Sandwich the edge of the A/strip set between the front and backing strips cut in step 6 with right sides together and the batting strip on the top of the front-side strip. Stitch the edges together; trim the batting close to the stitching as in step 4.

8. Press the strips away from the center and trim the ends and angle as in step 5.

9. Continue adding strips around the block, alternating widths and fabrics as desired until it is 14"–15" wide and 16"–18" long. Trim edges and square corners as needed to complete one rectangle-shape Crazy block.

10. Repeat steps 1–9 to complete a total of 16 Crazy Blocks. **Note:** *Blocks will not all be the same size.*

COMPLETING THE SASHING

1. Select four Crazy Blocks. Measure the total width of the blocks. Subtract this measurement from 64" to determine the total B sashing strips width needed.

2. Decide how wide you want to make each of the three B sashing strips, varying the widths as desired to total the amount needed. To each B strip width, add ¾" for seam allowances. **Note:** *If some blocks are shorter than others, add strips of sashing fabrics to the ends of the shorter blocks to make them all the same length as the longest block. Cut front, batting and backing strip for each set of strips as needed.*

3. Sew the first set of B sashing strips to the long edge of one block in the same manner as Completing the Blocks and as shown in Figure 4. **Note:** *The first seam uses a ¼" seam allowance.*

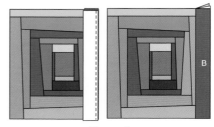

Figure 4

4. To add the next block, use a ½" seam allowance to sew the front side of the block to the right side of the front B sashing strip and batting layers only, leaving the backing strip free. Press the seam toward the B sashing strip.

5. Turn the raw edge of the backing sashing strip under ⅜" and apply fusible web tape along the edge as shown in Figure 5.

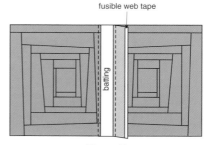

Figure 5

6. Overlap the fused edge over the ½" seam allowance on the stitched strips; fuse the edge in place.

7. From the front side, stitch in the ditch between the sashing and the block to secure the back-side sashing seam.

8. Repeat steps 3–7 to assemble the remaining selected blocks and short sashing strips to complete one row.

9. Repeat steps 1–8 to complete a total of four block rows.

10. Measure the combined length of the block rows and subtract from 84" to determine the finished width of the long sashing strips.

11. Prepare long sashing strips and join rows as in steps 2–7 to complete the quilt front and backing.

COMPLETING THE QUILT

1. Join the 2¼"-wide binding strips on the short ends with diagonal seams to make a 290"-long binding strip referring to Figure 6; trim seams to ¼" and press seams open.

Figure 6

2. Fold and press the binding strip with wrong sides together along length.

3. Leaving a 12" tail and matching raw edges of binding to raw edges of quilt, pin and stitch the binding strip to the right side of the quilt, mitering corners and overlapping at the beginning and end. Turn the binding strip to the back side to cover seam and hand- or machine-stitch in place to finish. ■

Crazy Blocks
Placement Diagram 64" x 80"

Easy Ragged Edges

This clever cutting technique makes it easy to create Log Cabin blocks in almost no time. The block is made using 10" squares of flannel or homespun.

DESIGN BY MERRY MAY

Make a Log Cabin block without all the fuss and the endless strips. A clever cutting technique will have you building these easy blocks in almost no time. The original block is based on using all 10" squares, so precut squares are ideal for the project.

Flannel or homespun fabrics are best because of their softness and ability to create a fluffy fringe when clipped, but you are not limited to using them.

The finished size of the block will end up being 1" smaller than the cut size, so it's easy to figure out the size of a project. A 10" cut square yields a 9" finished block.

Let's get to work and try one block using this technique.

MATERIALS

- 1 (4" x 4") A square
- 1 each light and dark 10" x 10" B square
- 1 (10" x 10") C square for back
- Neutral-color all-purpose thread
- Water-soluble fabric marker
- Basic sewing tools and supplies

COMPLETING THE BLOCKS

Note: *Use a ½" seam allowance throughout. Install a new needle and a walking foot on your sewing machine.*

1. Fold and crease each B square in half on one diagonal with folded edge at the bottom (photo 1).

2. Select one folded B square. Cut three 2" strips from the folded square starting at the folded edge, cutting longest strip first (photo 2).

3. Unfold the strips to reveal a square (A) and three L-shaped pieces (photo 3). Repeat with the second B square.

4. Begin by placing a C background square wrong side up on your work surface. Draw a large X on the square from corner to corner using a water-soluble fabric marker and a ruler.

5. Lay an A square right side up on top of the marked C square so each of the four corners of A align with the X lines (photo 4).

6. Select the shortest dark L-shaped strip; place it right side up on the marked C square with the three outer corners of the L matching the X lines and overlapping the A square (photo 5). Pin to hold in place.

7. Using the walking foot to measure a ½" seam allowance, sew along the inside edges of the L shape through all layers to the diagonal crease (photo 6); leave the needle in the fabric, lift the presser foot and turn a 90-degree corner to sew along second leg of L-shape. ***Note:*** *If you can't eyeball the correct distance for turning the corner by using the pressed diagonal crease, use a straightedge along the marked line through the center of the pieces to mark the stitching line and pivoting point for turning the fabric.*

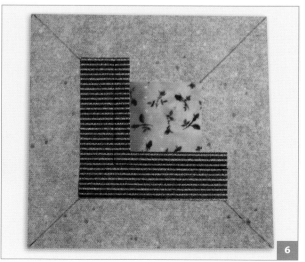

8. Place the shortest light L-shaped strip right side up on the opposite side of A/C, overlapping the previous stitched strip, again aligning the corners with the X lines on C (photo 8); sew this strip to C as in step 7.

9. Continue adding the L-shaped strips to C, alternating the darks and lights and aligning each new strip with the X lines on C until you have added three strips to each side of A (photos 9, 10 and 12). When you get to the outer set of strips, trim the first strip's short end so it is even with the top edge of the previous strip as shown in photo 11.

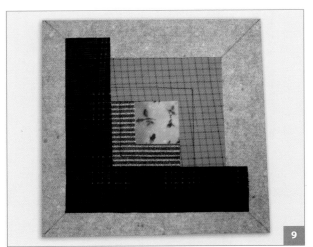

Last dark strip trimmed even with top edge of previous light strip.

10. Snip into the raw edges of each L-shaped strip every ⅛"–¼" toward the stitched seam line (photos 13 and 14); do not snip the outside edges at this time.

11. Once you have the blocks for your project sewn together, you will snip the rest of the seams, following the instructions for your project. Machine-wash and dry the block or completed project to make the raw edges "bloom." ***Note:*** *Be sure to check the lint filter on your dryer often to remove all of the built-up lint that will form during the drying process.* ■

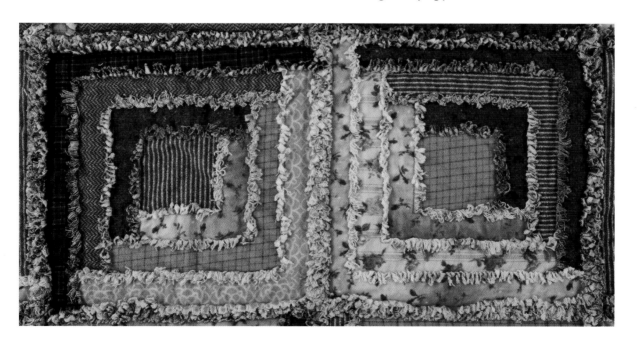

RAGGEDY LOG CABIN

When you finish sewing this quilt, there is no binding to add. Just snip the raw edges and toss it into the washer and dryer.

DESIGN BY MERRY MAY

PROJECT NOTE

Refer to page 36 for more in-depth instructions and photos for using this fun method of creating ragged-edge Log Cabin blocks.

PROJECT SPECIFICATIONS

Skill Level: Beginner
Quilt Size: 36" x 45"
Block Size: 9" x 9"
Number of Blocks: 20

MATERIALS

- ⅓ yard light or dark flannel or (20) 4" x 4" flannel squares for A
- ⅔ yard each of 4 different coordinating light fabrics
- ⅔ yard each of 4 different coordinating dark fabrics
- Neutral-color all-purpose thread
- Water-soluble fabric marker
- Basic sewing tools and supplies

CUTTING

1. Cut the A fabric into two 4" by fabric width strips; subcut strips into (20) 4" x 4" A squares.

2. Cut two 10" by fabric width strips from each of the light and dark fabrics; subcut a total of (60) 10" x 10" B squares from the strips. Set aside 20 squares for the background C squares.

COMPLETING THE BLOCKS

Note: *Use a ½" seam allowance throughout. Install a new needle and a walking foot on your sewing machine.*

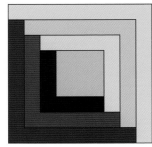

Ragged Edge Log Cabin
9" x 9" Block
Make 20

1. Fold and crease each B square in half on one diagonal with folded edge at the bottom as shown in Figure 1.

Figure 1   **Figure 2**

2. Cut three 2" strips from each folded square starting at the folded edge (cutting longest strips first) as shown in Figure 2.

3. Unfold the strips to reveal an A square and three L-shaped pieces as shown in Figure 3.

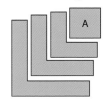

Figure 3

4. Repeat steps 2 and 3 with all B squares. ***Note:*** *Do not cut the set-aside C squares.*

5. Sort the L-shaped strips by size and in piles of lights and darks.

6. To complete one Ragged Edge Log Cabin block, begin by placing a C background square wrong side up on your work surface. Draw a large X on the square from corner to corner using a water-soluble fabric marker and a ruler as shown in Figure 4.

Figure 4 **Figure 5**

7. Lay an A square right side up on top of the marked C square so each of the four corners of A align with the X lines as shown in Figure 5.

Raggedy Log Cabin Throw
Placement Diagram 36" x 45"

8. Select one of the shortest dark L-shaped strips; place it on the C square with the three outermost corners of the L matching the X lines and overlapping the A square as shown in Figure 6. Pin to hold in place.

Figure 6

9. Using the walking foot to measure a ½" seam allowance, sew along one inside edge of the L shape through all layers, to the crease in the L shape corner; leaving the needle in the fabric, lift the presser foot and turn a 90-degree corner at the crease and sew second leg of L as shown in Figure 7. ***Note:*** *If you can't eyeball the correct distance for turning the corner, you may need to mark the ½" seam allowance on the piece before stitching.*

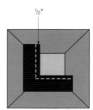

Figure 7

10. Place one of the shortest light L-shaped strips right side up on the opposite side of A/C, overlapping the previous stitched strip, again aligning the corners with the X lines on C as shown in Figure 8; sew this strip to C as in step 9.

Figure 8

11. Continue adding the L-shaped strips to C, alternating the darks and lights and aligning each new strip with the X lines on C until you have added three strips to each side of A as shown in Figure 9. When you get to the outer set of strips, trim the first strip's short end so it is even with the top edge of the previous strip as shown in Figure 10.

Figure 9

Figure 10

12. Snip into the raw edges of each L-shaped strip every ⅛"–¼" toward the stitched seam line as shown in Figure 11; do not snip the outside edges at this time.

Figure 11

13. Repeat steps 6–12 to complete a total of 20 Ragged Edge Log Cabin blocks.

COMPLETING THE QUILT

1. Arrange the blocks in five rows of four blocks each to make a pattern. *Note: Try different arrangements to determine the one you like. The sample uses the traditional Streak of Lightning Log Cabin layout.*

> **Tip**
>
> Take digital photos of each layout arrangement before making a decision. Take a look at them all at once to select your favorite.

2. Join the blocks in rows as arranged with the C squares right sides together and using a ½" seam allowance.

3. Join the rows as arranged with C pieces right sides together to complete the quilt piecing.

4. Sew ½" from the edge all around.

5. Snip into the raw edges of the blocks every ⅛"–¼" almost to the seams in between the blocks and the rows and outer edges.

6. Machine-wash and dry the quilt to make the raw edges "bloom." *Note: Be sure to check the lint filter on your dryer often to remove all of the built-up lint that will form during the drying process.* ■

> **Tip**
>
> Save the squares leftover from trimming the B squares to make a doll blanket to match the larger quilt. Simply layer two squares wrong sides together and sew together with a ½" seam allowance and clip into seams as for the quilt.

Folding & Pleating Strips

Folding fabric creates pleats and adds a layered, textured look to your Log Cabin blocks and to your project.

BY STEPHANIE SMITH

Precut 2½" by fabric width strips are the perfect choice to use when making a Log Cabin project. Some of the strips used in this method are folded to make a double layer, while other strips are folded and pleated to add another dimension to the finished project.

Although this block looks difficult and intimidating, making one sample block using this method takes it from intimidating to easy and fun.

Making One Folded Log Cabin Block

CUTTING

1. Cut one 4½" x 4½" square to use as a foundation, labeled F1. This can be muslin or white or cream tonal or mottled. It should be something that will not show through the layers that will be placed on top of it.

2. Cut one 2" x 2" square medium- or dark-colored fabric for the block center, labeled M1.

3. Cut one of each of the following lengths from 2½" x 42" precut light strips and fold the pieces with wrong sides together along the length to make a double-layered strip for round 1: 2½" L1 and 3" L2.

4. Repeat step 3 to make one of each length for round 2: 4½" L3 and 4½" L4.

5. Repeat step 3 with the 2½" precut dark strips for round 1: 3" D1 and 3½" D2.

6. Repeat step 3 with the 2½" precut dark strips for round 2: 4½" D3 and 4½" D4.

7. Cut the following from unfolded precut 2½" x 42" light strips: 4¾" L5, and 6¾" L6.

8. Cut the following from unfolded precut 2½" x 42" dark strips: 6¾" D5 and 8½" D6.

9. Cut the following strips for pleating from unfolded precut 2½" x 42" light strips: 8½" RL3 (finished length 4¾") and 12" (finished length 6¾") RL4.

10. Cut the following strips for pleating from unfolded precut 2½" x 42" dark strips: 12" RD3 (finished length 6¾") and 15" (finished length 8½") RD4.

PREPARING THE FOUNDATION BASE

1. Mark diagonal lines from corner to corner on the right side of the F1 foundation square using a pencil or marking pen. Then make a mark ¼" in from the corners of the square (photo 1).

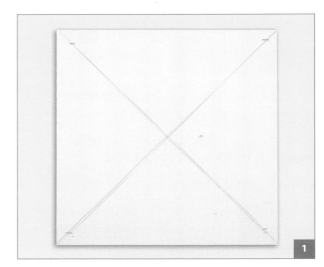

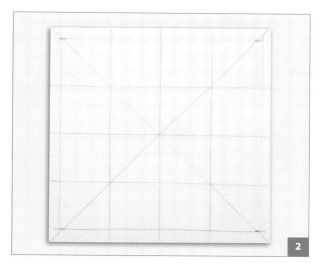

2. Mark 1" lines on each side of the square between the ¼" marks and connect the lines using a straight edge to make a grid (photo 2).

3. Using a pencil or marking pen of a different color, draw a line ½" from the center point on each side to help align strips (photo 3).

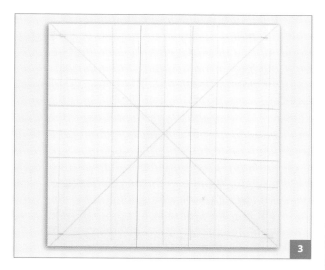

COMPLETING THE LOG CABIN BLOCK

1. Place the 2" x 2" M1 square right side up on the center of the F1 foundation square; pin in place. Stitch all around using a ¼" seam allowance (photo 4).

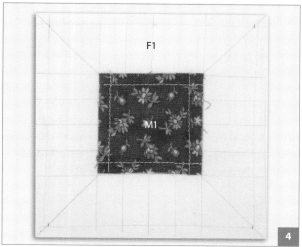

2. Align the folded edge of the L1 square with the previously marked ½" line, using the grid lines on the F1 foundation square to help you align in the correct position; stitch in place (photo 5).

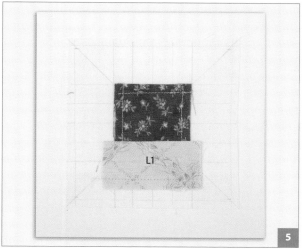

3. Add L2, D1 and D2 pieces to the F1 foundation square as in step 2 to complete round 1, using grid lines to align (photo 6). *Note: You should be using the line ½" away from the center mark, stitching each piece as it is placed.*

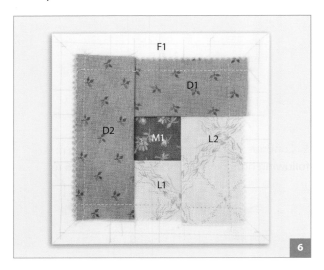

4. Align L3, L4, D3 and D4 pieces ½" away from the top edge of the first piece stitching in the first round using grid lines to help with positioning; stitch each piece in place as you go to complete round 2 of the Log Cabin unit (photos 7 and 8).

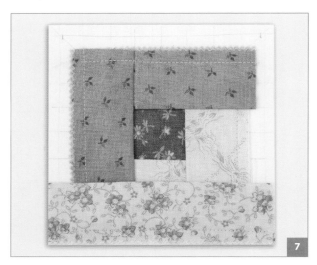

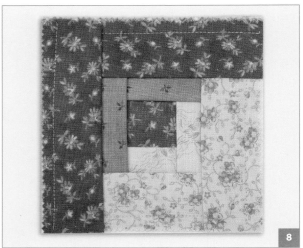

ADDING PLEATED STRIPS

1. Fold each R piece in half with wrong sides together along length and press.

2. Mark 1" increments on the back side of each folded strip near the raw edge for pleating. *Note: These marks will be used to align the folds to pleat to create ruffles (photo 9).*

Tip

It takes approximately 1½" –1¾" of fabric to make an inch of finished pleat. Add an extra inch to the beginning length of fabric strip prior to pleating to allow for placement of the pleat, if desired.

3. Select the marked RL3 strip; fold pleats by connecting the 1" marks together keeping the top edges of the folds flush; baste to hold in place. Place the strip on your sewing machine with the folded side up and the marked wrong side facing you. Stitch in place keeping the top edges of the folds flush (photo 10). *Note: Trim approximately ⅛" off the cut edge of the pleated strip once stitched. This will allow you to align and stitch the pleated strip into the Log Cabin block without seeing this seam once pressed open.*

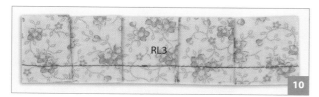

4. With wrong side facing up, align the edges of the RL3 edges with the L3 strip on the Log Cabin unit. Place the unfolded L5 strip right sides together on top of the ruffle; stitch in place (photo 11). *Note: The ruffle will be sandwiched between the Log Cabin unit and the L5 strip. Press L5 to the right side before adding the next strip.*

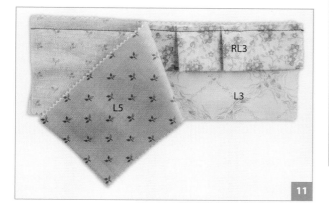

Tip

As you are folding, pinch pleat tightly to help align the 1" marks. You can use a straight pin to help you fold stiffer fabric.

Tip

When placing and stitching pleated strips into the Log Cabin block at right angles, it is helpful to use low-adhesive (painter's) tape to ensure proper alignment of the pleats.

When placing pleated strips, pay close attention to the orientation of the pleats so that they run in the same direction around the block.

5. Continue to add the strips and ruffle strips in the following order: RL4, L6, RD3, D5, RD4 and D6 to complete one Folded Log Cabin block (photo 12). ▪

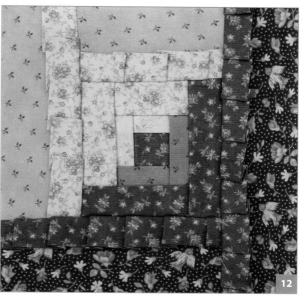

DESERT SUN PILLOW

Use folding techniques to add a textured look to the quartet of Log Cabin blocks that create this pillow. The sample was stitched with precut 2" strips, but yardage could also be used.

DESIGN BY STEPHANIE SMITH

PROJECT SPECIFICATIONS

Skill Level: Intermediate
Pillow Size: Approximately 24" x 24" without ruffle
Block Size: 12" x 12"
Number of Blocks: 4

MATERIALS

- 4 (2" x 2") squares dark purple mottled for M1 pieces
- 20 precut 2½" x 42" strips coordinating dark brown fabrics
- 20 precut 2½" x 42" strips coordinating cream/light brown fabrics
- 1 fat quarter cream tonal
- ⅜ yard gold solid
- ⅞ yard coordinating batik
- Cream, tan and brown all-purpose thread
- 28 ounces polyester fiberfill
- Pencil or marking pen
- Straightedge
- Low-adhesive painter's tape
- Basic sewing tools and supplies

PROJECT NOTES

The size of the blocks or finished pillow may be altered by adding or removing strips or increasing/decreasing the width of the strips used.

CUTTING

1. Cut four 4½" x 4½" A squares cream tonal for foundations.

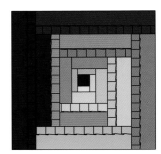

Log Cabin
12" x 12" Block
Make 4

2. Cut four 2½" by fabric width strips gold solid for M2 ruffles.

3. Select two each 2½" x 42" light and two dark strips for each block. Fold each strip with wrong sides together along length and press to make double-layered strips.

4. Subcut folded strips as follows for round 1: 2½" light L1, 3" light L2, 3" dark D1 and 3½" dark D2.

5. Subcut folded strips into two 4½" light strips for L3 and L4 and two 4½" dark strips for D3 and D4 for round 2.

6. From the remaining unfolded 2½" x 42" precut light strips, cut the following: 4¾" L5, 6¾" L6, 8¾" L7 and 10¾" L8.

7. From the remaining unfolded 2½" x 42" precut dark strips, cut the following: 6¾" D5, 8½" D6, 10¾" D7 and 12½" D8.

8. Select two 2½" x 42" dark strips for D7 and D8 ruffle strips.

9. Cut the following light strips for pleating from the 2½" x 42" precut light strips: 8½" RL3, 12" RL4, 15½" RL7 and 19" RL8.

10. Cut the following dark strips for pleating from the 2½" x 42" precut dark strips: 12" RD3, 15" RD4, 19" RD7 and 22" RD8.

11. Cut one 24½" x 24½" backing piece from the coordinating batik.

COMPLETING THE BLOCKS

1. To complete one Desert Sun block, mark the A foundation square on each diagonal using a pencil or marking pen; mark ¼" from the corners of the square as shown in Figure 1.

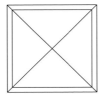

Figure 1

2. Mark a 1" grid on the foundation square, referring to red lines in Figure 2. Mark a line ½" from the center point on each side to help align strips in the proper position, referring to blue lines in Figure 2.

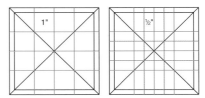

Figure 2

3. Pin and stitch an M1 square right side up on the center of A as shown in Figure 3.

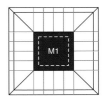

Figure 3

4. Align the folded edge of an L1 piece with the ½" line marked in step 2, using the grid lines on the foundation to help you align the fabric correctly as shown in Figure 4; stitch in place along the raw edge. **Note:** *The folded edge is left open.*

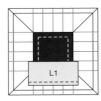

| Figure 4 | Figure 5 |

5. Continue to add strips L2, D1 and D2 pieces on A as in step 4 to complete round 1 as shown in Figure 5. **Note:** *The L1, L2, D1 and D2 strips may all be placed, pinned and stitched in one step, if desired.*

6. Aligning raw edges of L3, L4, D3 and D4 pieces with raw edges of foundation A, stitch in place individually to complete round 2 as shown in Figure 6.

Figure 6

7. Select a folded RL3 strip; mark 1" increments on the back side of the strip near the raw edge. **Note:** *It takes approximately 1½"–1¾" of fabric to make a 1" finished ruffle. Add an extra inch to the beginning length of fabric prior to pleating to allow for placement of ruffle, if desired.*

8. Select the marked RL3 strip; fold pleats by connecting the 1" marks together keeping the top edges of the folds flush; baste to hold in place. Place the strip on your sewing machine with the folded side up and the marked wrong side facing you. Stitch in place keeping the top edges of the folds even when you stitch as shown in Figure 7. **Note:** *Trim approximately ⅛" off the cut edge of the pleated strip once stitched. This will allow you to align and stitch the pleated strip into the Log Cabin block without seeing this seam once pressed open.*

Figure 7

9. Align and pin the edges of the RL3 strip even with the edges of an L5 strip right sides together as shown in Figure 8.

Figure 8

10. Place the pinned RL3/L5 strip right sides together on the L3 side of a Log Cabin unit, aligning edges, and stitch as shown in Figure 9. **Note:** *The pleated layer will be sandwiched between the Log Cabin block and the L5 strip. Press the L5 strip to the right side.*

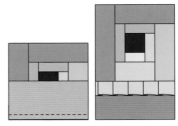

Figure 9

11. Complete the third round around the Log Cabin unit using the RL4, L6; RD3, D5; RD4 and D6 strips as shown in Figure 10.

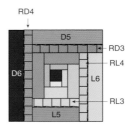

Figure 10

12. Complete the fourth round around the Log Cabin unit using the RL7, L7; RL8, L8; RD7, D7; RD8 and D8 pieces as shown in Figure 11.

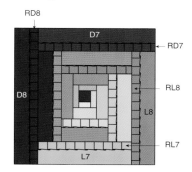

Figure 11

13. Repeat steps 1–12 to make a total of four Log Cabin blocks.

COMPLETING THE PILLOW TOP

1. Place a D7 and M2 strip right sides together; stitch both ends and along one long side; turn right side out. Press flat so that approximately ⅛" of contrasting fabric is visible as shown in Figure 12; repeat to make two D7/M2 strips.

Figure 12

2. Repeat step 1 with D8 and M2 to make two D8/M2 strips.

3. Mark the M2 side of the strip in 1" increments using a pencil or marking pen.

4. Align marks, pin and baste pleats in each of the strips; trim approximately ⅛" off the raw edge.

5. Join two Log Cabin blocks to make a row as shown in Figure 13; press seam to one side. Repeat to make two rows. Join the rows to complete the pillow top, referring to the Placement Diagram; press seam to one side.

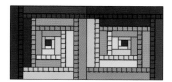

Figure 13

6. Pin a pleated ruffle strip right sides together to each side of the pillow top; stitch in place.

7. Place the backing square right sides together with the pillow top; stitch all around, leaving a 6" opening on one side. Clip corners; turn right side out through the opening.

8. Insert polyester fiberfill to desired fullness.

9. Turn opening edges in ¼"; hand-stitch opening closed.

10. Hand-stitch pleated ruffles together at each corner, as shown in Figure 14, to finish. ∎

Figure 14

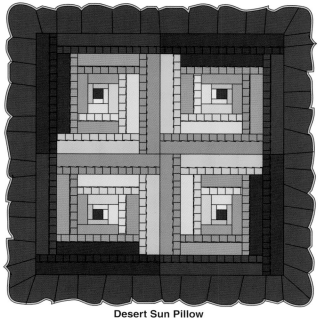

Desert Sun Pillow
Placement Diagram Approximately 24" x 24" without ruffle

Paper Piecing From the Top

This technique may be a little difficult for a beginner, but someone experienced with the Log Cabin block will like this method. It's fast and very accurate.

BY SANDRA L. HATCH

USING FOUNDATION OR PAPER PIECING

For many years, I have avoided paper piecing. I tried it once and really did not like trying to cut pieces that would turn into the shapes of the stitched pieces.

I also know that paper piecing is the best and most accurate method to use when precise piecing of narrow points is required or when tiny pieces that are impossible to cut, nevermind sew, are used.

About 20 years ago, I saw an antique navy-and-white Pineapple-patterned quilt and fell in love—I wanted to duplicate that quilt. I took some slides of it, went home and drew out a pattern, bought the fabric and set out to piece some blocks.

I used the old-fashioned template method in the beginning—that did not yield accurate results (photo 1). I tried cutting strips, sewing them around the center and trimming the excess; the result was a square that was not square (photo 2).

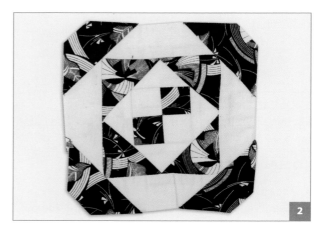

I was discouraged, so I packed it all up and put it away. Now, 20 years later, I have decided to try once again with paper piecing from the top side. This method is working for me and my blocks are absolutely perfect!

Foundation piecing from the top side is not a new method. Quilters have used it since the early days when making crazy quilts or Log Cabin quilts. The fabric pieces were placed on a fabric foundation and stitched in place to add stability. When the piecing was finished, the excess was trimmed to match the foundation piece, making every block the same size.

When quilters wanted to use this method on paper to yield accurate results, some adjustments had to be made.

The pattern begins in the center with a scant 2½" square (photo 3). **Note:** *In the sample, the center square is a pieced Four-Patch unit.* The square is pinned inside the drawn square. Note that now the center square includes the seam allowance.

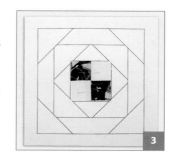

The first strip to surround the center square is aligned right sides together with the center square and with the 2½" line on the paper and stitched a perfect ¼" away from the line (photo 4). Note that the red extending lines on the paper show an extension of the line in both directions (photo 5). These lines give a starting point for beginning and ending the stitching. When folded to the right side, the strip should be close to, but not touching, the line on the paper.

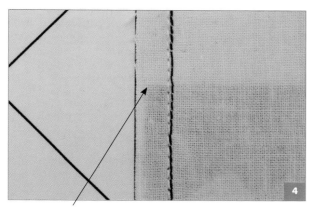

¼-inch seam allowance

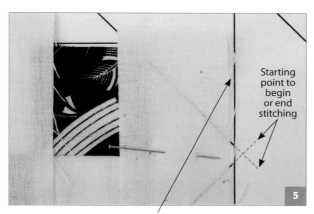

Strip is close, but not touching the line.

What if the piece is too small and does not nearly meet the line? No problem! As long as it is within the ¼" seam allowance, it will work just fine (photo 6). It should not be more than ⅛" from the line because that will leave a very narrow seam allowance on the

finished block, but the wonderful thing about this method is that even if the piece is not perfectly aligned with the marked line on the foundation, the finished block will still be perfect if you are using an accurate ¼" seam allowance as you sew.

Piece is small and doesn't meet the line, but it is within the seam allowance.

What if the piece extends beyond the line? That will make it hard to use the line for the guide for stitching on the next piece. I trimmed any little bit that extends beyond the line (photo 7).

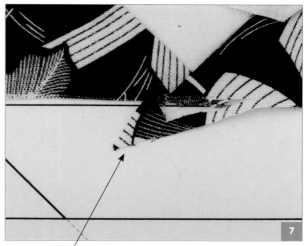

Trim material that extends beyond the line.

In the sample project, Pineapple Four-Patch on page 57, just two fabrics are used—one light and one dark. Sometimes the dark shows through to the light side; wherever that happens, I trimmed off the dark fabric. Those little points that extend on the dark triangles must be trimmed on those blocks because they show through. If using darker fabrics, or fabrics that won't show through, that trimming is not necessary.

The most important thing to remember when paper piecing from the top side is to use a very accurate ¼" seam allowance when stitching. This may be accomplished in several ways. My sewing machine allows me to move the needle in small increments. I was able to set the needle ¼" away from the edge of the presser foot, which guaranteed me a perfect ¼" seam allowance every time.

Other options include installing a ¼" presser foot on your machine. Many of the newer sewing machines include a ¼" foot, but if not, you may purchase one for a reasonable price. They are available for all machine models and were developed by a quilter, for a quilter. They are available online or through most quilt shops.

By gathering the few items listed to make a Pineapple block sample, let's get started trying foundation or paper piecing from the top side.

MATERIALS

- 1 scant 2½" x 2½" square dark fabric
- 2 (1½" x 42") light strips
- 1 (2⅞" x 42") dark strip
- Tracing paper
- Light thread
- ¼" presser foot or sewing machine with moveable needle
- Scissors

MAKING THE PATTERNS

1. Trace the pattern given on pages 62 and 63 to make one full-size pattern. **Note:** *You may make a photocopy, but be sure the copied pattern is the exact same size as the one given here in this book.*

2. Cut the 2⅞" x 42" strip into 2⅞" squares. Cut each square in half on one diagonal to make triangles.

Tip

When multiple patterns are needed, tracing can get tiresome. To help save time and effort, after tracing a couple of patterns, layer four or five pieces of tracing paper with one traced copy and staple edges to hold together.

Using your sewing machine, stitch on the marked lines to make perforated lines through all layers. Remove the staples and use these perforated copies as patterns. Instead of aligning fabric pieces with the lines, use the stitching lines as guides.

If you find this does not work for you, you may trace along the stitched lines to mark. This is quicker than trying to trace accurately because the line is already there to follow!

3. Set machine stitch length at 1.8 or 14–16 stitches per inch. This will help make removing paper easier when the block is complete.

4. Pin the scant 2½" x 2½" square in the center of the paper-piecing pattern. It must be scant because it should not cover the lines for the square in the center of the pattern (photo 3).

5. Place a 1½" x 42" strip right sides together with the center square, extending the beginning end past the square (photo 8).

6. Start stitching at the end line, aligning the edge of the presser foot with the line extension and the marked line to the end of the seam (photo 9). ***Note:*** *When sewing light fabrics, it is easy to see through the fabric to find the starting or stopping points. If you have trouble finding those when stitching, mark with a pen or marker as needed.*

7. Fold the strip to the right side and finger-press flat; pin in the center to hold. Fold over each end to the angled line and crease; trim excess along creased line (photo 10).

8. Repeat steps 5–7 to add one round of 1½"-wide strips around the center (photo 11).

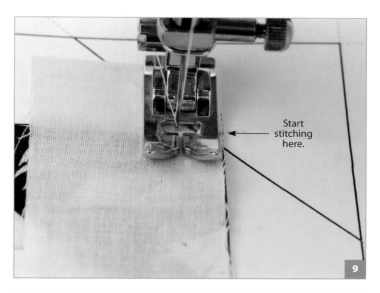

Start stitching here.

9

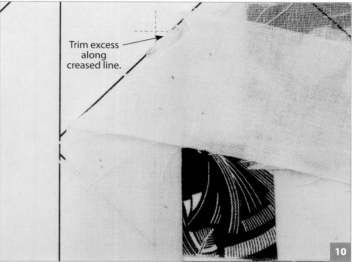

Trim excess along creased line.

10

Making Templates

If you prefer to work with exact-size pieces, make two copies of the paper-piecing pattern. Cut one of them up on the lines to make a template for each size piece. Cut pieces from the 1½"-wide strips using the templates. You will need four of each size for the 1½"-wide pieces. The 2⅞" x 42" strips are cut to make the triangles, so no template is needed for those.

11

9. Fold each triangle and crease to mark the diagonal center. Center the crease right sides together on a strip at the cross marks on one corner of the pieced section. Stitch ¼" from the marked line (photo 12). Fold the triangle to the right side and finger-press flat (photo 13); pin to hold. Trim triangle ends even with the line (photo 14). *Note: Move pins from previous round to the corners so that you are using the same pins over and over again.*

10. Continue adding strips, and then triangles, until you reach the outer line to complete the block (photo 15). Do not remove paper until the blocks are stitched together, matching the outer lines of the paper. ***Note:*** *You may remove the inner area of the paper, leaving just the outer rows for removal after piecing the top (photo 16). This allows you to iron the center parts of the block before joining into rows, if desired.* ■

Front of completed block.

Triangle ends need trimming.

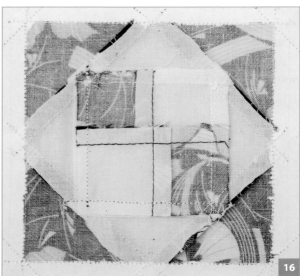

Back of completed block.

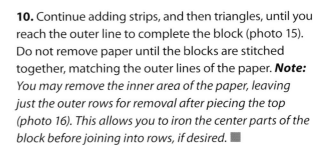

Triangle ends trimmed.

PINEAPPLE FOUR-PATCH

The Pineapple Log Cabin block is well known, but still very unique. Non-quilters do not look at the block in a quilt like this and instantly know that it is a Log Cabin design. This design is also unique in the technique that is used to make it. Once you learn the paper-piecing-from-the-top technique, you'll discover that it is very easy and very accurate. It does, however, require an experienced quilter to understand and learn this unique paper-piecing technique.

DESIGNED & PIECED BY SANDRA L. HATCH
MACHINE-QUILTED BY SANDY BOOBAR

PROJECT NOTES

The Pineapple Four-Patch blocks in this quilt were paper-pieced from the top side. Refer to page 52 for further instructions for using this method of paper piecing.

PROJECT SPECIFICATIONS

Skill Level: Intermediate
Quilt Size: 90" x 100"
Block Size: 10" x 10"
Number of Blocks: 56

MATERIALS

- 6 yards navy-with-white print
- 8 yards unbleached muslin
- Batting 98" x 108"
- Backing 98" x 108"
- All-purpose thread to match fabrics
- Paper for paper piecing
- Basic sewing tools and supplies

CUTTING

1. Cut (10) 1½" by fabric width A strips navy-with-white print.

Pineapple Four-Patch
10" x 10" Block
Make 56

2. Cut (32) 2⅞" by fabric width strips navy-with-white print; subcut strips into (448) 2⅞" squares. Cut each square in half on one diagonal to make 896 D triangles.

3. Cut two 6½" x 88½" O strips and two 6½" x 90½" P strips along the length of the navy-with-white print.

4. Cut the remaining width of the navy-with-white print fabric into 2¼"-wide strips to total at least 392" for binding. **Note:** *If you prefer to cut fabric width strips you will need (10) 2¼" by fabric width strips or ¾ yard of fabric for binding.*

5. Cut (10) 1½" by fabric width B strips unbleached muslin.

6. Cut (155) 1½" by fabric width strips unbleached muslin for pieces C, E, F and G.

7. Cut (16) 1½" by fabric width strips unbleached muslin. Join strips on short ends to make one long strip; press seams open. Subcut strip into two each of the following lengths: 80½" H, 72½" I, 86½" M and 78½" N.

8. Cut six 2½" by fabric width strips unbleached muslin; subcut strips into (72) 2½" J squares and two each 6½" K and 4½" L rectangles.

COMPLETING THE A-B FOUR-PATCH UNITS

1. Sew an A strip to a B strip with right sides together along length to make an A-B strip set; press seam toward A. Repeat to make a total of 10 A-B strip sets.

2. Subcut the A-B strip sets into (264) 1½" A-B segments as shown in Figure 1.

Figure 1

3. Select two A-B segments and join as shown in Figure 2 to complete one A-B unit; press seam to one side. Repeat to make a total of 132 A-B units.

Figure 2

COMPLETING THE BLOCKS

1. Select one A-B unit, 16 D triangles, three 1½"-wide fabric width strips unbleached muslin and one prepared paper foundation pattern.

2. Pin the A-B unit to the center of the marked side of the paper pattern as shown in Figure 3. **Note:** *You should be able to see the marked line on the paper around the edges of the unit.*

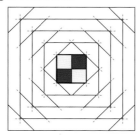

Figure 3

3. Place and pin a 1½"-wide strip unbleached muslin right sides together with the A-B unit, aligning one long edge along the marked line around the A-B unit and extending on the beginning end about ½" as shown in Figure 4.

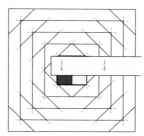

Figure 4

4. Set machine for 1.8–2.0 or 18–20 stitches per inch. Stitch a seam ¼" from the marked line as shown in Figure 5.

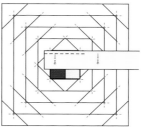

Figure 5

5. Finger-press the strip to the right side and trim excess along the marked line as shown in Figure 6.

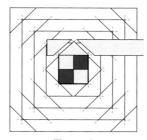

Figure 6

6. Repeat steps 3–5 to complete one C round around the center A-B unit as shown in Figure 7.

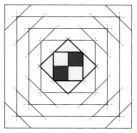

Figure 7

7. Center and pin a D triangle along the marked line on one side of the stitched center as shown in Figure 8. **Note:** *The marked line on the paper should not be covered by the piece. You should be able to see it to use as a guide to stitch a perfect ¼" seam.*

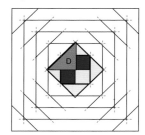

Figure 8

8. Finger-press D to the right side and trim even with the marked lines, if necessary.

9. Continue to add D to each side of the stitched center to complete the D round as shown in Figure 9.

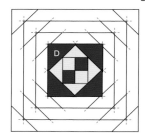

Figure 9

10. Continue to add strips and D triangles around the block until you have completed the block; trim excess paper and finish strips up to the marked line, but do not cut away the line.

11. Repeat steps 1–10, using strips and trimmed portions of strips, to complete a total of 56 Pineapple Four-Patch blocks.

12. Leaving the outer round of paper, remove paper backing from all blocks; trim threads as necessary. **Note:** *You may leave the paper on the blocks until the entire pieced center is stitched, but it will be very bulky to sew. You may also remove the paper from the last round, if desired. If the blocks are accurately pieced, sewing them together without relying on the paper for accuracy makes for easier stitching.*

COMPLETING THE QUILT

1. Select seven Pineapple Four-Patch blocks. Join blocks to complete an X row as shown in Figure 10; press seams in one direction. Repeat to make four X rows. **Note:** *Pay close attention to the orientation of the A-B Four-Patch units in the center of each block when joining blocks in rows.*

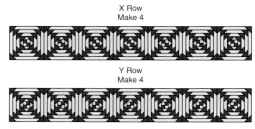

Figure 10

2. Select seven Pineapple Four-Patch blocks. Join blocks to complete a Y row, again referring to Figure 10. Repeat to make four Y rows.

3. Join the rows beginning with an X row and referring to the Placement Diagram for positioning; press

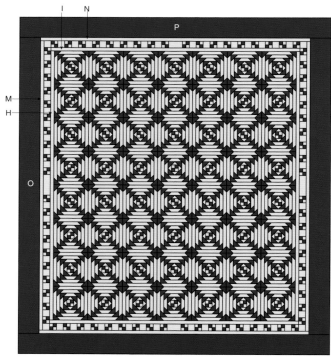

Pineapple Four-Patch
Placement Diagram 90" x 100"

seams in one direction. **Note:** *Pay close attention to the orientation of the A-B Four-Patch units in the rows when joining rows.*

4. Sew an H strip to opposite long sides and I strips to the top and bottom of the pieced center; press seams toward H and I strips.

5. Join 10 A-B units with nine J squares to make a long A-B-J strip as shown in Figure 11; press seams toward J. Repeat to make four long A-B-J strips. **Note:** *Pay close attention to the orientation of the A-B units in the strips when piecing.*

Figure 11

6. Join two long A-B-J strips with a K rectangle to make a side strip as shown in Figure 12; press seams toward K. Repeat to make a second side strip.

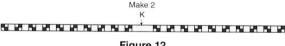

Figure 12

7. Sew a side strip to opposite long sides of the pieced center referring to the Placement Diagram for orientation of the strips; press seams toward H strips.

8. Join nine each A-B units and J squares to make a short A-B-J strip as shown in Figure 13; press seams toward J squares. Repeat to make four short A-B-J strips.

Figure 13

9. Join two short A-B-J strips with an L rectangle to make a top strip as shown in Figure 14; press seams toward L. Repeat to make the bottom strip.

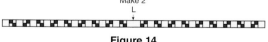

Figure 14

10. Sew the top strip to the top and bottom strip to the bottom of the pieced center referring to the Placement Diagram for orientation of the strips; press seams toward I strips.

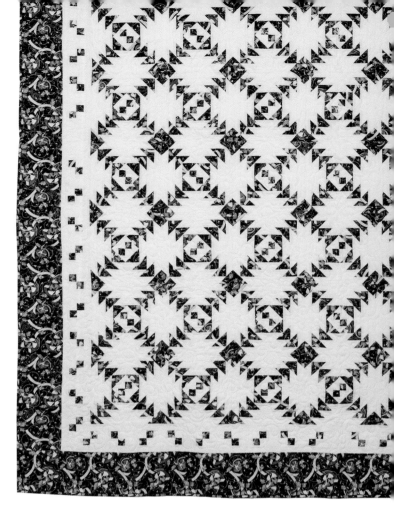

11. Sew M strips to opposite long sides and N strips to the top and bottom of the pieced center; press seams toward M and N strips.

12. Sew O strips to opposite long sides and P strips to the top and bottom of the pieced center to complete the pieced top; press seams toward O and P strips.

13. Layer, quilt and bind referring to Finishing Your Quilt on page 175. ∎

Designer Tip

Apply a fray preventative to the wrong side of the blocks after removing paper and trimming threads to prevent further fraying while working with the blocks.

When a light-colored fabric such as muslin is used with a dark fabric, threads might show through after quilting. Cutting down on fraying helps to reduce this problem.

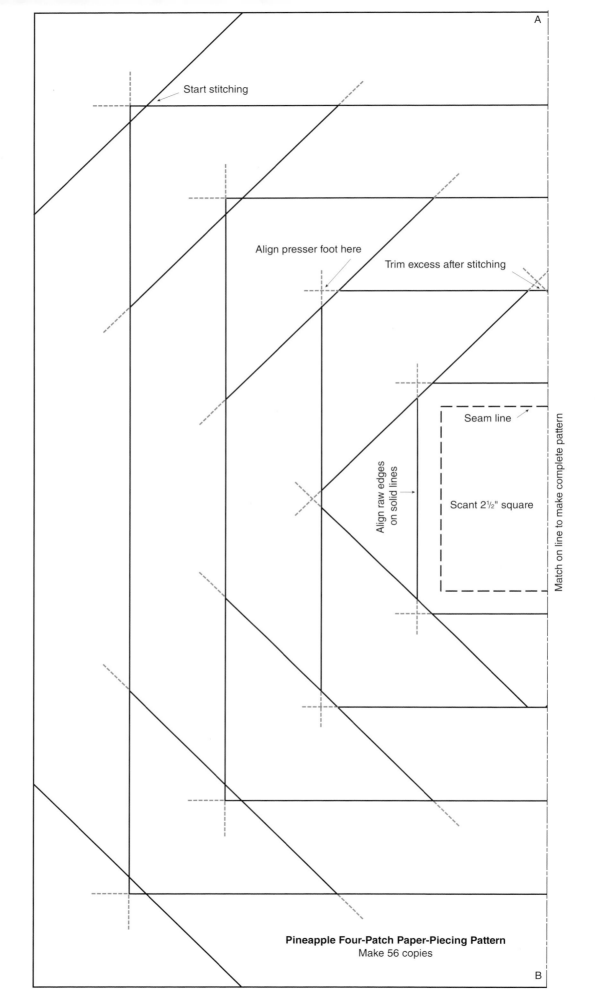

A

B

Start stitching

Align presser foot here

Trim excess after stitching

Seam line

Align raw edges on solid lines

Scant 2½" square

Match on line to make complete pattern

Pineapple Four-Patch Paper-Piecing Pattern
Make 56 copies

B

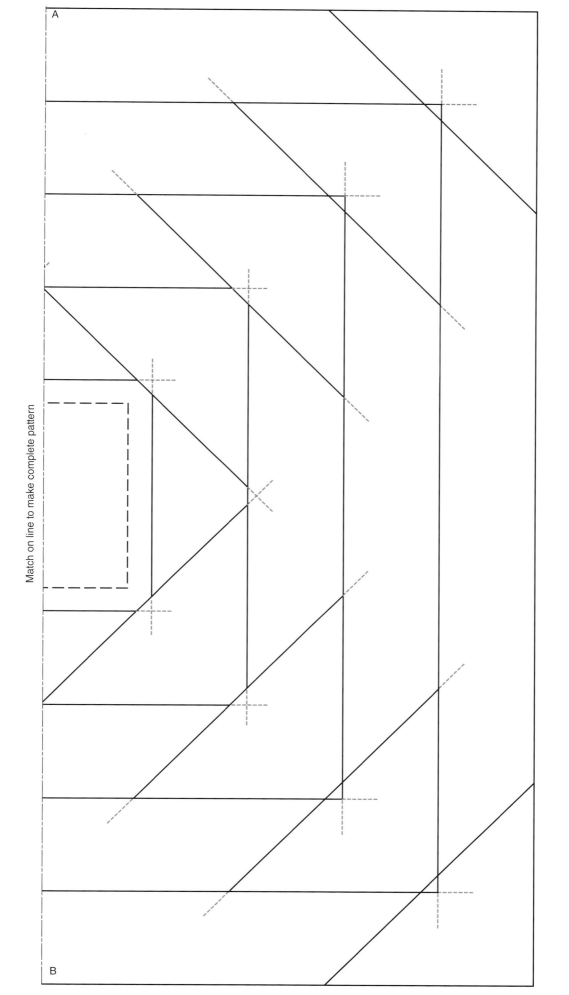

A

B

Match on line to make complete pattern

EVERY WHICH WAY

Combine Chevron Log Cabin blocks and Mariner's Compass blocks to create this scrappy bed quilt. It will really reduce your fabric stash.

DESIGN BY NORMA STORM

PROJECT NOTES

The fabrics used in the Mariner's Compass blocks may be a mixture of solids, tonals, mottleds, batiks or prints. The most important part of the fabric selection process is to find three different values of fabric in the same color family for each combination except the red/blue blocks, of which there are two different versions. These blocks used red for the B pieces and two different blue fabrics for the A and C pieces. Either scraps or a planned purchase of fat quarters in different color families results in beautiful blocks.

PROJECT SPECIFICATIONS

Skill Level: Advanced
Quilt Size: 85" x 109"
Block Size: 12" x 12" and 6" x 6"
Number of Blocks: 35 and 56

MATERIALS

- Large variety of light and dark scraps cut 2" wide
- 1 fat quarter each light, medium and dark fabrics in the following colors: orange, red, purple, turquoise, green, yellow, peach, rose, blue and red/blue fabrics
- ⅝ yard blue floral
- 2 yards white tonal
- 4 yards navy solid
- Batting 93" x 117"
- Backing 93" x 117"
- Neutral-color all-purpose thread
- Quilting thread
- Template material
- Basic sewing tools and supplies

Chevron Quarter
6" x 6" Block
Make 56

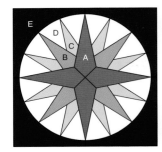

Mariner's Compass
12" x 12" Block
Make 17

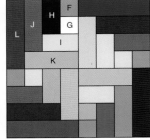

Chevron Log Cabin
12" x 12" Block
Make 18

CUTTING

1. Cut seven 2" by fabric width strips blue floral; subcut strips into (128) 2" F squares.

2. Select a variety of 2" light strips; subcut these strips into a total of (128) 2" G squares.

3. Sort the remainder of the 2"-wide strips into lights and darks; place the lights into one bag and the darks into another for random selection later. ***Note:*** *If you prefer to cut the individual pieces to the exact size, see the Precise Cutting sidebar on page 68 for specific sizes.*

4. Prepare templates A–E using patterns given; cut as directed on each piece. Transfer dots and other markings and cutting information to the templates.

5. Cut eight 3½" by fabric width M/N strips white tonal. Join strips on short ends to make one long strip; press seams open. Subcut strip into two 60½" M strips and two 90½" N strips.

6. Cut nine 4" by fabric width O/P strips navy solid. Join strips on short ends to make one long strip; press seams open. Subcut strip into two 78½" O strips and two 109½" P strips.

7. Cut (10) 2¼" by fabric width strips navy solid for binding.

COMPLETING THE CHEVRON LOG CABIN & QUARTER CHEVRON BLOCKS

1. Sew an F square to a G square to make an F-G unit; press seam toward F.

2. Select a 2"-wide dark strip for H; place H right sides together on the F-G unit with the F square on top as shown in Figure 1; stitch a ¼" seam; open to the right side and press seam toward H. Turn the unit over with the H side on the bottom and trim H ends even with the F-G unit as shown in Figure 2.

Figure 1   Figure 2

3. Select a 2"-wide light strip for I; repeat step 2 to complete a round on just two sides of the F-G unit as shown in Figure 3.

Figure 3

4. Continue adding the dark J and L strips and the light K strip to complete one Chevron Quarter block referring to Figure 4 for positioning; measure and trim the completed block to 6½" x 6½", if necessary.

Figure 4

5. Repeat steps 1–4 to complete a total of 128 Chevron Quarter blocks; set aside 56 blocks for borders.

6. Select four Chevron Quarter blocks.

7. Join two blocks to make a row, alternating placement of the F corners as shown in Figure 5; press seam to one side. Repeat to make a second row.

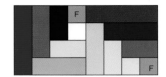

Figure 5

8. Turn one row and join to complete one Chevron Log Cabin block referring to Figure 6; press seam to one side.

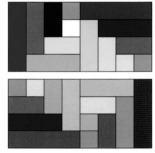

Figure 6

9. Repeat steps 6–8 to complete a total of 18 Chevron Log Cabin blocks.

COMPLETING THE MARINER'S COMPASS BLOCKS

1. Select four each matching color family A and B pieces and eight matching color family C pieces, 16 D pieces and four E pieces for one block.

2. Sew C between two D pieces, starting stitching at the dots and stitching to the opposite end of each seam to make a C-D unit as shown in Figure 7; press seams away from C. Repeat to make a total of eight C-D units.

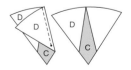

Figure 7

3. Sew a C-D unit to opposite sides of B to make a B-C-D unit, matching the marked lines on B to assure proper placement as shown in Figure 8; press seams toward the C-D units. Repeat to make four B-C-D units.

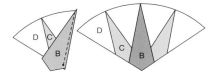

Figure 8

4. Center and sew E to each B-C-D unit to make B-C-D-E units as shown in Figure 9; press seams toward E.

Figure 9

5. Join two A pieces, stitching from dot to dot as shown in Figure 10; press seam to one side. Repeat to make two A units.

Figure 10

6. Join the two A units as in step 4 to complete the center unit as shown in Figure 10; press seam in one direction.

7. Set the B-C-D-E units into the spaces between the A units, starting at the inside dots and stitching to the outside edge on each side to complete one Mariner's Compass block, again referring to Figure 11.

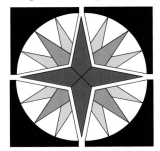

Figure 11

8. Repeat steps 1–7 to complete a total of 17 blocks— one each rose, blue and peach and two each turquoise, orange, green, yellow, red, purple and blue/red.

COMPLETING THE QUILT

1. Arrange and join two Mariner's Compass blocks with three Chevron Log Cabin blocks to make an X row referring to Figure 12; press seams toward the Chevron Log Cabin blocks. Repeat to make four X rows.
Note: *Place Mariner's Compass blocks in a pleasing arrangement by color across the quilt top referring to the Placement Diagram for positioning.*

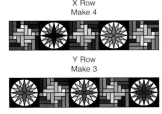

Figure 12

2. Arrange and join two Chevron Log Cabin blocks with three Mariner's Compass blocks to make a Y row, again referring to Figure 12; press seams toward the Chevron Log Cabin blocks. Repeat to make three Y rows. **Note:** *Place Mariner's Compass blocks in a pleasing arrangement by color across the quilt top referring to the Placement Diagram for positioning.*

3. Join the rows, beginning with an X row and alternating the X and Y rows, to complete the pieced center; press seams in one direction.

4. Sew the M strips to the top and bottom and N strips to opposite long sides of the pieced center; press seams toward M and N strips.

Precise Cutting Log Strips From Scraps

To cut exact-size rectangles for the Chevron Log Cabin and Chevron Quarter blocks, cut 128 each of the following sizes from the 2"-wide scrap strips.

Lights–3½" I and 5" K
Darks–3½" H, 5" J and 6½" L

5. Arrange and join 15 Chevron Quarter blocks, alternating the placement of the F corner squares in blocks from side to side as shown in Figure 13 to make a side border strip; press seams in one direction. Repeat to make a second side border strip.

Figure 13

6. Sew a side border strip to opposite long sides of the pieced center referring to the Placement Diagram for positioning of strips; press seams toward N strips.

7. Repeat step 4 with 13 Chevron Quarter blocks each to make the top and bottom border strips. Sew these border strips to the top and bottom of the pieced center, again referring to the Placement Diagram for positioning of strips; press seams toward M strips.

8. Sew an O strip to the top and bottom and P strips to opposite long sides of the pieced center to complete the quilt top; press seams toward O and P strips.

9. Layer, quilt and bind referring to Finishing Your Quilt on page 175. ■

Every Which Way
Placement Diagram 85" x 109"

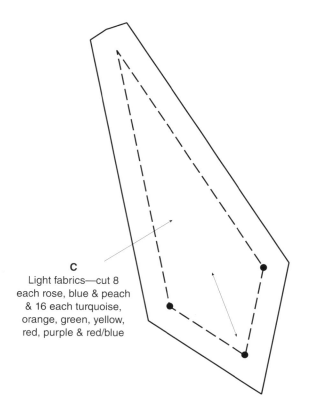

C
Light fabrics—cut 8
each rose, blue & peach
& 16 each turquoise,
orange, green, yellow,
red, purple & red/blue

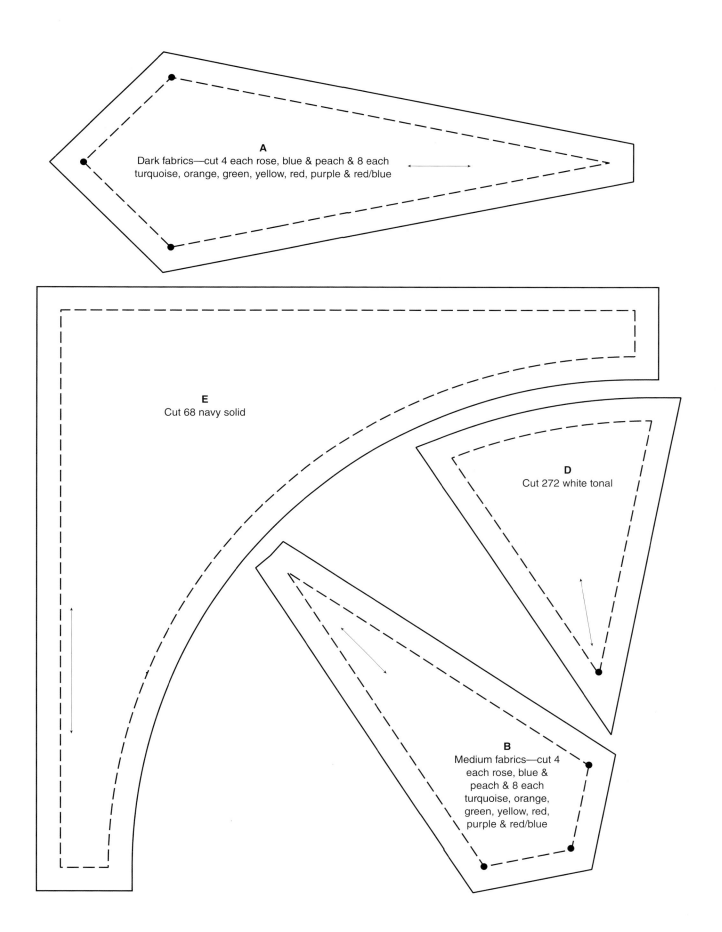

A

Dark fabrics—cut 4 each rose, blue & peach & 8 each turquoise, orange, green, yellow, red, purple & red/blue

E

Cut 68 navy solid

D

Cut 272 white tonal

B

Medium fabrics—cut 4 each rose, blue & peach & 8 each turquoise, orange, green, yellow, red, purple & red/blue

LIGHTS IN THE CABIN

Find 28 different pieces of fabric, one for each lantern, to create this scrappy throw. Use the Courthouse Steps Log Cabin variation for a fun, easy project.

DESIGN BY JUDITH SANDSTROM

PROJECT NOTES

Fabric placement in the blocks of this quilt is essential to the creation of the lantern shapes. The fabric on one side of one block must match the fabric on one side of the next block in the row to create the design. Careful planning before cutting and during construction is the best way to guarantee a successful result.

PROJECT SPECIFICATIONS

Skill Level: Intermediate
Quilt Size: 55" x 55"
Block Size: 10" x 10" and 10" x 5"
Number of Blocks: 23 and 4

MATERIALS

- ¼ yard each 28 bright solids, tonals or scraps
- ¼ yard black tonal
- ½ yard blue mottled
- ⅝ yard orange dot
- 1¼ yards white tonal
- Batting 63" x 63"
- Backing 63" x 63"
- Neutral-color all-purpose thread
- Quilting thread
- Basic sewing tools and supplies

CUTTING

1. Cut three 3" by fabric width strips white tonal; subcut strips into (54) 1¾" B pieces.

2. Cut two 5½" by fabric width strips white tonal; subcut strips into (46) 1¾" D pieces.

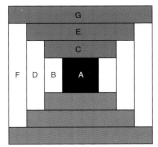

Courthouse Steps
10" x 10" Block
Make 23

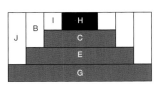

Half Courthouse Steps
10" x 5" Block
Make 4

3. Cut two 8" by fabric width strips white tonal; subcut strips into (46) 1¾" F pieces.

4. Cut two 1¾" by fabric width strips white tonal; subcut strips into eight each 1¾" I squares and 4¼" J pieces.

5. Cut two 3" by fabric width strips black tonal; subcut strips into (23) 3" A squares and four 1¾" x 3" H rectangles.

6. Cut two 1¾" by fabric width strips from each of the bright fabrics; subcut each fabric strip into two rectangles each as follows: 5½" C, 8" E and 10½" G. *Note: Some fabrics will only be used once.*

7. Cut six 3" by fabric width strips orange dot. Join strips on short ends to make one long strip; press seams open. Subcut strips into two 50½" K strips and two 55½" L strips.

8. Cut six 2¼" by fabric width strips blue mottled for binding.

COMPLETING THE COURTHOUSE STEPS BLOCKS

1. To complete one Courthouse Steps block, select one each C, E and G strip of two different fabrics. Select two each B, D and F strips and one A square.

2. Sew a B strip to opposite sides of A as shown in Figure 1; press seams toward B.

Figure 1

Figure 2

3. Sew a different color C strip to the remaining opposite sides of A as shown in Figure 2; press seams toward C.

4. Continue to add strips to opposite sides of the center unit in alphabetical order referring to Figure 3 for color placement; press seams toward strips as added. **Note:** *Two different fabrics are used on the colored sides of each block. It is best to decide the color layout before starting, and then plan the cutting and strip placement in each block to create the lantern design.*

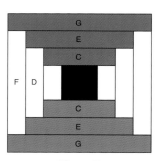
Figure 3

X row
Make 3

Figure 4

5. Using one bright color from the previous block and one new color, repeat steps 1–4 to complete a total of five Courthouse Steps blocks for one X row, laying out the blocks and pinning together to make the X row as shown in Figure 4.

6. Repeat steps 1–5 to complete two more sets of five blocks to make two more X rows referring to the Placement Diagram for color positioning.

7. Repeat steps 1–5 to make two sets of four Courthouse Steps blocks to make two partial Y rows referring to Figure 5 and the Placement Diagram for color positioning.

Partial
Y row
Make 2

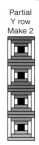
Figure 5

COMPLETING THE HALF COURTHOUSE STEPS BLOCKS

1. To complete one Half Courthouse Steps block, select one each H, C, E and G strip and two each B, I and J strips. **Note:** *The C, E and G fabrics should be the same as the top and bottom colors in each of the partial Y rows, again referring to Figure 4 for color positioning.*

2. Sew I to opposite short ends of H and add C as shown in Figure 6; press seams toward I and C.

Figure 6

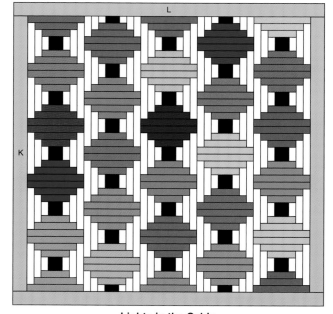
Lights in the Cabin
Placement Diagram 55" x 55"

3. Continue to add pieces to the pieced unit as shown in Figure 7 to complete one Half Courthouse Steps block; press seams toward strips as added.

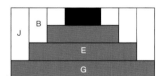

Figure 7

4. Repeat steps 1–3 to complete a total of four Half Courthouse Steps blocks.

COMPLETING THE QUILT

1. Stitch the pinned blocks in the X rows to complete three X rows referring to Figure 8.

2. Pin a Half-Log Cabin block to each end of each pinned Y row and stitch the blocks together to complete two Y rows, again referring to Figure 8.

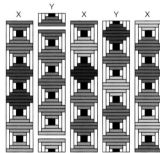

Figure 8

3. When satisfied with the block/row arrangement, join the blocks in rows; press seams in adjacent rows in opposite directions.

4. Join the rows to complete the pieced center; press seams in one direction.

5. Sew a K strip to opposite sides and L strips to the top and bottom of the quilt center to complete the pieced top; press seams toward K and L strips.

6. Layer, quilt and bind referring to Finishing Your Quilt on page 175. ■

AUTUMN HUES QUARTER BLOCKS

Collect your autumn fabric, including small scraps, and create Log Cabin blocks one quarter at a time. Before you add the sashing and sew the blocks together, try out several settings for just the right look.

DESIGN BY WENDY SHEPPARD

PROJECT SPECIFICATIONS

Skill Level: Beginner
Quilt Size: 42½" x 51½"
Block Size: 8" x 8"
Number of Blocks: 20

MATERIALS

- Orange fabric scraps to total ¼ yard
- Yellow/gold fabric scraps to total ½ yard
- Green fabric scraps to total ¾ yard
- Red fabric scraps to total 1 yard
- ⅞ yard green-with-white dots
- ⅞ yard cream solid
- Batting 51" x 60"
- Backing 51" x 60"
- Neutral-color all-purpose thread
- Quilting thread
- Basic sewing tools and supplies

CUTTING

1. Cut (20) 2½" x 2½" A squares orange fabrics.

2. Cut 20 each 2½" x 2½" B squares and 2½" x 4½" C rectangles yellow/gold fabrics.

3. Cut 20 each 2½" x 4½" D and 2½" x 6½" E rectangles green fabrics.

4. Cut 20 each 2½" x 6½" F and 2½" x 8½" G rectangles from red fabrics.

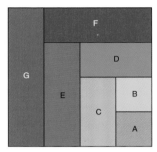

Autumn Hues
8" x 8" Block
Make 20

5. Cut (12) 1½" x 1½" I squares red fabrics.

6. Cut two 8½" by fabric width strips cream solid; subcut strips into (31) 1½" H sashing strips.

7. Cut two 1¾" x 35½" J strips cream solid.

8. Cut three 1¾" by fabric width strips cream solid. Join strips on short ends to make one long strip; press seams open. Subcut strip into two 47" K strips.

9. Cut two 3" x 43" M strips green-with-white dots.

10. Cut three 3" by fabric width strips green-with-white dots. Join strips on short ends to make one long strip; press seams open. Subcut strip into two 47" L strips.

11. Cut five 2¼" by fabric width strips green-with-white dots for binding.

COMPLETING THE BLOCKS

1. To complete one Autumn Hues block, select one each A, B, C, D, E, F and G piece from different fabrics.

2. Sew A to B; press B to the right side with seam toward B.

3. Add C to the left side edge of the A-B unit as shown in Figure 1; press C to the right side with seam toward C.

Figure 1

4. Continue to add pieces to the A-B-C unit in alphabetical order referring to Figure 2, pressing seams toward the most recently added rectangles, to complete one Autumn Hues block.

Figure 2

5. Repeat steps 1–4 to complete a total of 20 Autumn Hues blocks.

COMPLETING THE QUILT

1. Join four Autumn Hues blocks with three H strips to make a block row referring to the Placement Diagram

for positioning of blocks. ***Note:*** *You may arrange the blocks as you desire to change the look of the completed quilt. Figure 3 shows an alternate setting.*

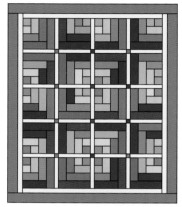

Figure 3

2. Repeat step 1 to make five block rows; press seams toward H strips.

3. Join three I squares with four H strips to make a sashing row as shown in Figure 4; press seams toward H strips. Repeat to make a total of four sashing rows.

Figure 4

4. Join the block rows with the sashing rows, beginning and ending with the block rows, to complete the pieced center; press seams toward sashing rows.

5. Sew J strips to the top and bottom and K strips to opposite long sides of the pieced center; press seams toward J and K strips.

6. Sew the L strips to opposite long sides and M strips to the top and bottom of the pieced center to complete the quilt top; press seams toward the L and M strips.

7. Layer, quilt and bind referring to Finishing Your Quilt on page 175. ■

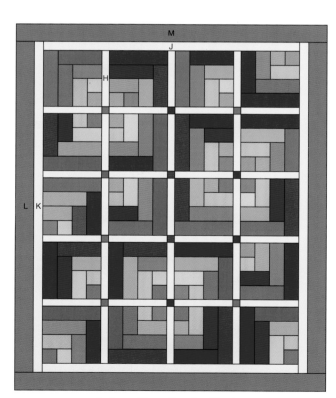

Autumn Hues Quarter Blocks
Placement Diagram 42½" x 51½"

TRIANGLE BEGINNINGS

Select leftover fabric from a recent project or scraps from your stash to create a colorful bed runner. Half-square triangles in the center and strips of different widths make it unique.

DESIGN BY PHYLLIS DOBBS

PROJECT SPECIFICATIONS

Skill Level: Beginner
Quilt Size: 92" x 32"
Block Size: 12" x 12"
Number of Blocks: 14

MATERIALS

- ⅛ yard green leopard print
- ⅛ yard pink leopard print
- ¼ yard pink zebra print
- ⅓ yard green/plum print
- ⅜ yard cream/green geometric print
- ⅜ yard purple print
- ½ yard pink geometric print
- ⅝ yard fuchsia floral
- ⅝ yard green zebra print
- ⅝ yard pink floral
- ¾ yard cream/green floral
- 1¼ yards plum/green print
- Batting 100" x 40"
- Backing 100" x 40"
- Neutral-color all-purpose thread
- Quilting thread
- Basic sewing tools and supplies

CUTTING

1. Cut one 6⅜" by fabric width strip green/plum print; subcut strip into two 6⅜" A squares and four 1¾" x 6" B strips. Cut each A square in half on one diagonal to make four A triangles; discard one.

2. Cut one 6⅜" by fabric width strip purple print; subcut strip into one 6⅜" A square, four 2¼" x 8¾"

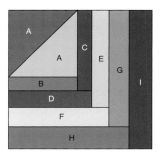

Triangle Beginnings
12" x 12" Block
Make 14

F strips and five 2" x 7¼" D strips. Cut the A square in half on one diagonal to make two A triangles.

3. Cut one 2½" by fabric width strip purple print; subcut strip into three 10½" H strips.

4. Cut one 6⅜" by fabric width strip plum/green print; subcut strip into two 6⅜" A squares and two 8¾" x 2½" F strips. Cut the A squares in half on one diagonal to make four A triangles.

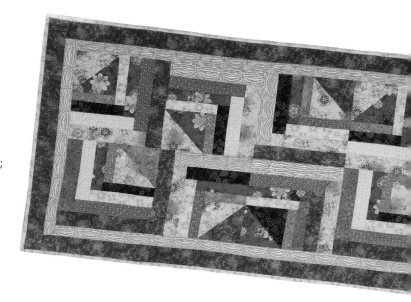

5. Cut one 12½" by fabric width strip plum/green print; subcut strip into (10) 2½" I strips.

6. Cut six 3" by fabric width strips plum/green print. Join strips on short ends to make one long strip; press seams open. Subcut strip into two 87½" L strips and two 32½" M strips.

7. Cut one 6⅜" by fabric width strip pink floral; subcut strip into six 6⅜" A squares. Cut each square in half on one diagonal to make 12 A triangles.

8. Cut one 10½" by fabric width strip pink floral; subcut strip into seven 2½" H strips and four 2¼" G strips.

9. Cut one 6⅜" by fabric width strip fuchsia floral; subcut strip into four 6⅜" A squares. Cut each square in half on one diagonal to make eight A triangles; discard one.

10. Cut one 8¾" by fabric width strip fuchsia floral; subcut strip into seven 2" E strips. Trim remainder of strip to 7¼" and subcut into seven 2" D strips.

11. Cut one 8¾" by fabric width strip cream/green floral print; subcut strip into seven 2" E strips. Trim remainder of strip to 7¼" and subcut into seven 1¾" C strips.

12. Cut six 2¼" by fabric width binding strips cream/green floral print.

13. Cut six 2" by fabric width strips green zebra print. Join strips on short ends to make one long strip; press seams open. Subcut strip into two 84½" J strips and two 27½" K strips.

14. Cut one 2½" by fabric width strip green zebra print; subcut strip into four 10½" H strips.

15. Cut two 1¾" by fabric width strips green leopard print; subcut strip into (10) 6" B strips.

16. Cut one 8¾" by fabric width strip cream/green geometric print; subcut strip into eight 2¼" F strips.

17. Cut two 2½" by fabric width strips pink zebra print; subcut strips into four 12½" I strips.

18. Cut one 2" by fabric width strip pink leopard print; subcut strip into two 7¼" D strips. Trim remainder of strip to 1¾" wide; subcut into three 7¼" C strips.

19. Cut one 10½" by fabric width strip pink geometric print; subcut strip into (10) 2¼" G strips. Trim remainder of strip to 7¼" and cut four 1¾" C strips.

COMPLETING THE BLOCKS

1. Stack all same-lettered/size strips together—you should have 28 A triangles and 14 of each size B–I pieces.

2. Select two A triangles and one each of the other letters (B–I) for one block. Mix up the colors so you only have the same fabric in the block once.

3. Sew A to A along the diagonal to make a square as shown in Figure 1; press seam to one side.

Figure 1   **Figure 2**

4. Sew a B strip to the A unit as shown in Figure 2; press seam toward B.

5. Sew C to the right edge of the same A triangle as shown in Figure 3; press seam toward C.

Figure 3

6. Continue to add pieces to the B and C sides of the unit in alphabetical order to complete one Triangle Beginnings block referring to Figure 4; press seams toward strips as added.

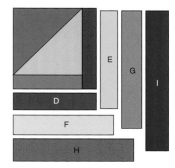

Figure 4

7. Repeat steps 2–6 to complete a total of 14 Triangle Beginnings blocks referring to the Placement Diagram and the photo of the sample quilt for color-placement suggestions.

COMPLETING THE QUILT

1. Select seven Triangle Beginnings blocks and join to make a row referring to the Placement Diagram for positioning suggestions; press seams in one direction. Repeat to make a second row, pressing seams in the opposite direction.

2. Join the rows to complete the pieced center; press seam in one direction.

3. Sew a J strip to opposite long sides and K strips to each end of the pieced center; press seams toward J and K strips.

4. Sew an L strip to opposite long sides and M strips to each end of the pieced center to complete the quilt top; press seams toward L and M strips.

5. Layer, quilt and bind referring to Finishing Your Quilt on page 175. ■

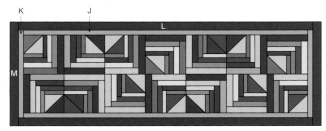

Triangle Beginnings
Placement Diagram 92" x 32"

BASKET OF FLOWERS

Use two sizes of triangles in the middle to create baskets using the traditional piecing method. Before the weekend is over, your quilt top will be finished.

DESIGN BY CHRIS MALONE

PROJECT SPECIFICATIONS

Skill Level: Beginner
Quilt Size: 70" x 86"
Block Size: 14" x 14"
Number of Blocks: 20

MATERIALS

Note: *Fabric requirements based on 42½" useable fabric width.*
- ¼ yard medium brown tonal
- ⅓ yard pink tonal
- ⅝ yard dark brown print
- ¾ yard multicolored brown floral
- 1 yard brown/green stripe
- 1¼ yards green print
- 1¼ yards brown/tan print
- 1½ yards white dot
- 1¾ yards red small floral
- Batting 78" x 94"
- Backing 78" x 94"
- Neutral-color all-purpose thread
- Quilting thread
- Ruler with ¹⁄₁₆" marks and 45-degree marked angle
- Basic sewing tools and supplies

CUTTING

1. Cut two 10⁹⁄₁₆" by fabric width strips multicolored brown floral; subcut strips into five 10⁹⁄₁₆" squares. Cut each square on both diagonals to make a total of 20 A triangles.

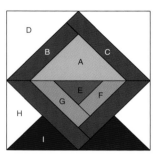

Basket of Flowers
14" x 14" Block
Make 20

2. Cut two 9⅛" by fabric width strips brown/tan print; subcut strips into (40) 2⅛" B strips. With right side up, cut left end of each strip on a 45-degree angle as shown in Figure 1 to make angled B pieces. ***Note:*** *It is important to cut the pieces exactly as shown in Figure 1 for pieces to be placed correctly in the blocks.*

Figure 1

3. Cut two 10¾" by fabric width strips brown/tan print; subcut strips into (40) 2⅛" C strips. With right side up, cut right end of each strip on a 45-degree angle as shown in Figure 2 to make angled C pieces. ***Note:*** *It is important to cut the pieces exactly as shown in Figure 2 for pieces to be placed correctly in the blocks.*

Figure 2

4. Cut four 7⅞" by fabric width strips white dot; subcut strips into (20) 7⅞" squares. Cut each square in half on one diagonal to make 40 D triangles.

5. Cut two 8³⁄₁₆" by fabric width strips white dot; subcut strips into (10) 8³⁄₁₆" squares. Cut each square on both diagonals to make 40 H triangles.

6. Cut one 6" by fabric width strip medium brown tonal; subcut strip into five 6" squares. Cut each square on both diagonals to make 20 E triangles.

7. Cut two 5¹³⁄₁₆" strips brown/green stripe; subcut strip into 20 identical 2⅛" F rectangles, centering stripe in each rectangle. With right side up, cut left end of each strip on a 45-degree angle as shown in Figure 3 to make angled F pieces. ***Note:*** *It is important to cut the pieces exactly as shown in Figure 3 for pieces to be placed correctly in the blocks.*

Figure 3

8. Cut two 7⁷⁄₁₆" strips brown/green stripe; subcut strip into 20 identical 2⅛" G rectangles, centering stripe in each rectangle. With right side up, cut right end of each strip on a 45-degree angle as shown in Figure 4 to make angled G pieces. ***Note:*** *It is important to cut the pieces exactly as shown in Figure 4 for pieces to be placed correctly in the blocks.*

Figure 4

9. Cut two 8³⁄₁₆" by fabric width strips dark brown print; subcut strips into (10) 8³⁄₁₆" squares. Cut each square on both diagonals to make 40 I triangles.

10. Cut four 14½" by fabric width strips red small floral; subcut strips into (49) 2½" K strips.

11. Cut three 2½" by fabric width strips pink tonal; subcut strips into (34) 2½" J squares.

12. Cut eight 2½" by fabric width strips green print. Join strips on short ends to make one long strip; press seams open. Subcut strip into two 82½" L and two 66½" M strips.

13. Cut eight 2¼" by fabric width strips green print for binding.

COMPLETING THE BLOCKS

1. To complete one Basket of Flowers block, sew B to the left short side and C to the right short side of A as shown in Figure 5; press seams toward B and C pieces.

Figure 5

2. Sew D to the B and C sides of A to complete the basket top as shown in Figure 6; press seams toward D.

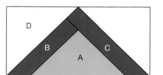

Figure 6

Basket of Flowers
Placement Diagram 70" x 86"

3. Sew F to one short side and G to the other short side of E as shown in Figure 7; press seams toward F and G.

Figure 7

4. Add B to the F side and C to the G side of the E-F-G unit to make a B-C-E-F-G unit as shown in Figure 8; press seams toward B and C.

Figure 8

5. Sew I to H to make an I-H unit as shown in Figure 9; press seam toward H. Repeat to make a reverse I-H unit, again referring to Figure 9.

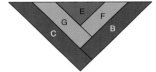

Figure 9

6. Sew the I-H and reverse I-H units to the B-C-E-F-G unit to complete one basket bottom as shown in Figure 10; press seams toward the I-H and reverse I-H units.

Figure 10

7. Sew the basket top to the basket bottom to complete one Basket of Flowers block referring to the block drawing; press seam toward basket top.

8. Repeat steps 1–7 to complete a total of 20 Basket of Flowers blocks.

COMPLETING THE QUILT

1. Join four Basket of Flowers blocks with five K sashing strips to make a block row as shown in Figure 11; press seams toward K strips. Repeat to make five block rows.

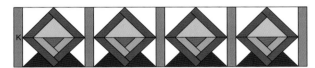

Figure 11

2. Join four K sashing strips with five J sashing squares to make a sashing row as shown in Figure 12; press seams toward the K sashing strips. Repeat to make six sashing rows.

Figure 12

3. Join the block rows with the sashing rows, beginning and ending with the sashing rows, to complete the pieced center; press seams toward sashing rows.

4. Sew L strips to opposite long sides of the pieced center; press seams toward L strips.

5. Sew a J square to each end of each M strip; press seams toward M.

6. Sew the J-M strips to the top and bottom of the pieced center to complete the pieced top; press seams toward M strips.

7. Layer, quilt and bind referring to Finishing Your Quilt on page 175. ◼

ROSE CABIN COASTERS

These coasters can be made in an hour or two, even by a beginner. Stitch a small Log Cabin block, add a leaf and the coaster is finished.

DESIGN BY CHRIS MALONE

PROJECT SPECIFICATIONS

Skill Level: Beginner
Coaster Size: 4" x 4" without leaf
Block Size: 4" x 4"
Number of Blocks: 4

MATERIALS FOR 4 COASTERS

- Scraps yellow
- 4 different pink scraps
- 4 different red scraps
- 7" x 14" rectangle green tonal
- 4 backing squares 4½" x 4½"
- 4 batting squares 4½" x 4½"
- 1 batting rectangle 3½" x 14"
- All-purpose thread to match fabric
- No. 8 pearl cotton: pink, red, dark green and yellow
- Embroidery needle
- Basic sewing tools and supplies

CUTTING

1. Cut four 1½" x 1½" A squares yellow scraps.

2. Cut four each of the following: 1¼" x 1½" B strips pink scrap 1, 1¼" x 2¼" C strips pink scrap 2, 1¼" x 2¼" D strips pink scrap 3 and 1¼" x 3" E strips pink scrap 4.

3. Cut four each of the following: 1¼" x 3" F strip red scrap 1, 1¼" x 3¾" G strip red scrap 2, 1¼" x 3¾" H strip red scrap 3 and 1¼" x 4½" I strip red scrap 4.

COMPLETING THE LEAVES

1. Trace the leaf pattern four times on the wrong side of one end of the green tonal rectangle, leaving ⅜" between pieces when tracing.

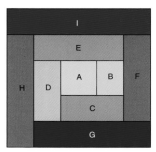

Log Cabin
4" x 4" Block
Make 4

2. Fold the fabric rectangle in half right sides together to make a double layer; pin to the strip of batting.

3. Sew around each drawn leaf shape through all layers, leaving bottom edges open as shown in Figure 1.

Figure 1

4. Cut out each stitched leaf shape ⅛" from seam; trim leaf tip and batting close to seam. Turn leaf shapes right side out; press flat.

5. Transfer vein lines to leaf shapes.

6. Using green pearl cotton, straight-stitch on the marked lines to complete the leaves.

COMPLETING THE BLOCKS

1. To complete one Log Cabin block, select one of each pieces A–I.

2. Sew B to A; press seam toward B.

3. Sew C to the A-B unit referring to Figure 2; press seam toward C.

Figure 2

4. Continue to add pieces around the A-B-C unit in alphabetical order referring to Figure 3 to complete one Log Cabin block, pressing seams toward the most recently added piece as you sew.

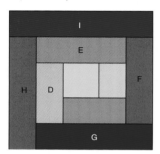

Figure 3

5. Repeat steps 1–4 to complete a total of four Log Cabin blocks.

COMPLETING THE COASTERS

1. To complete one coaster, place a leaf shape right sides together on one Log Cabin block matching straight edges as shown in Figure 4; baste in place.

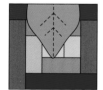

Figure 4

2. Place a backing square right sides together on the basted Log Cabin/leaf unit; pin the layers to a batting square.

3. Stitch all around the layered unit, leaving 2½" open on one side; clip corners and trim batting close to seam.

4. Turn right side out through the opening; press flat.

5. Turn opening edges inside ¼"; hand-stitch opening closed.

6. Using red pearl cotton, quilt through the center of the B/C/D/E strips as shown in Figure 5.

7. Using pink pearl cotton, quilt through the center of the F/G/H/I strips as in step 6.

8. Using yellow pearl cotton, add seven French knots in the center of each A square to finish.

9. Repeat steps 1–8 to complete a total of four Rose Cabin Coasters. ■

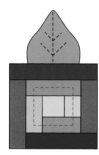

Figure 5

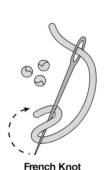

French Knot

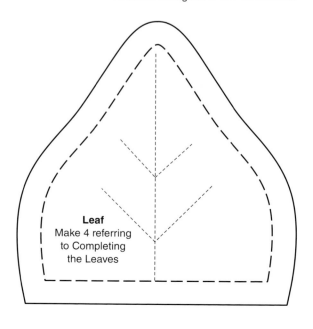

Rose Cabin Coasters
Placement Diagram 4" x 4" without leaf

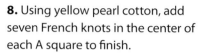

Leaf
Make 4 referring to Completing the Leaves

CARVED IN STONE PLACE MAT

Paper-piecing two sizes of Log Cabin blocks makes this a quick weekend project.

DESIGN BY CONNIE KAUFFMAN

PROJECT NOTES

For more in-depth and complete step-by-step instructions for paper-piecing Log Cabin blocks, turn to page 14.

PROJECT SPECIFICATIONS

Skill Level: Beginner
Place Mat Size: 18½" x 12"
Block Sizes: 4" x 4" and 7⅜" x 7⅜"
Number of Blocks: 6 and 1

MATERIALS FOR 2 PLACE MATS

- ⅓ yard white marbled print
- ½ yard black marbled print
- ⅔ yard brown/black marbled print (includes backing)
- 2 batting rectangles 19" x 12½"
- All-purpose thread to match fabric
- Quilting thread
- Basic sewing tools and supplies

CUTTING

1. Cut two 2" by fabric width strips black marbled print for pieces F, G, H and I.

2. Cut six 1" by fabric width strips black marbled print for pieces K, M, N, P, S, U and V.

3. Cut two 1¼" by fabric width strips black marbled print; subcut strip into four 11" X strips.

4. Cut one 2" by fabric width strip white marbled print for pieces B, C, D and E.

Left-End Log
4" x 4" Block
Make 3

Right-End Log
4" x 4" Block
Make 3

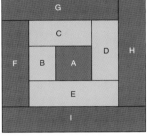

Center Log
7⅜" x 7⅜" Block
Make 1

5. Cut five 1" by fabric width strips white marbled print for pieces J, L, O, Q, R and T.

6. Cut one 6⅛" by fabric width strip brown/black marbled print; subcut strip into four 6⅛" W squares and two 2½" x 2½" A squares. Cut each W square in half on one diagonal to make eight W triangles.

7. Cut two 19" x 12½" backing squares brown/black marbled print.

COMPLETING THE BLOCKS

1. Make six copies each of the Right-End Log and Left-End Log patterns and two copies of the Center Log pattern.

2. To begin making one Center Log block, center and pin the A square right side up on the unprinted side of one copy of the paper pattern over the space marked for A.

3. Place a B strip right side down on top of the A square. The edge of the B strip should be even with the left edge of A as shown in Figure 1.

Figure 1

4. Set your machine to a very close stitch (18–20 stitches per inch) so that the paper will tear away from the sewing lines easier later.

5. Hold or pin the pieces together; turn over and sew along the line between pieces A and B, starting stitching ¼" from the line and ending ¼" past the line.

6. Trim the excess length of the B strip even with the A square as shown in Figure 2. Fold the B piece to the right side and finger-press flat. Pin to hold in place.

Figure 2

7. Select the C strip and repeat steps 5 and 6, aligning the edge of the C strip even with the A/B strips.

8. Continue to add all strips in this same manner to complete two Center Log blocks and six each Right-End Log and Left-End Log blocks to make two place mats.

9. Trim all blocks on the outside solid lines.

COMPLETING THE PLACE MATS

1. To complete one place mat, sew a W triangle to each side of one Center Log block; press seams toward W.

2. Sew an X strip to the top and bottom of the W/block unit to complete the center unit as shown in Figure 3; press seams toward X strips.

Figure 3

3. Join three Right-End Log blocks to make a right-end strip as shown in Figure 4; press seams in one direction. Repeat with three Left-End

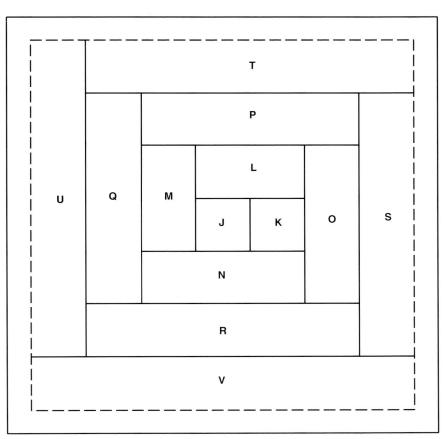

Left-End Log Paper-Piecing Pattern
Make 3 copies

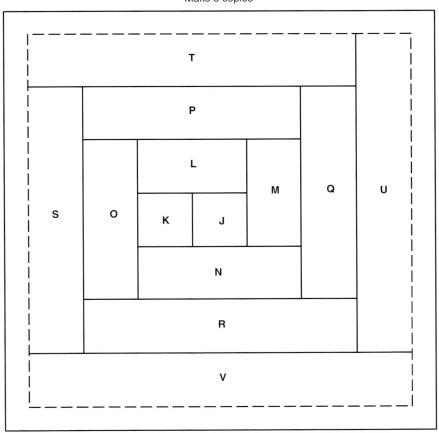

Right-End Log Paper-Piecing Pattern
Make 3 copies

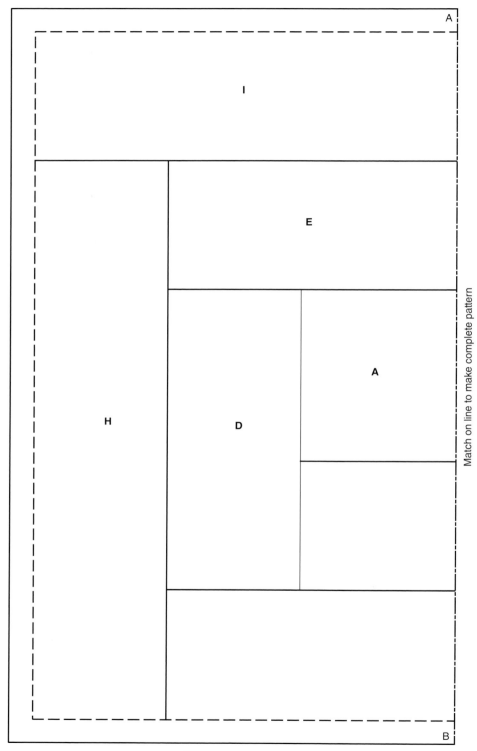

A

Match on line to make complete pattern

I

E

H

D

A

B

Paper-Piecing Pattern
Make 1 copy

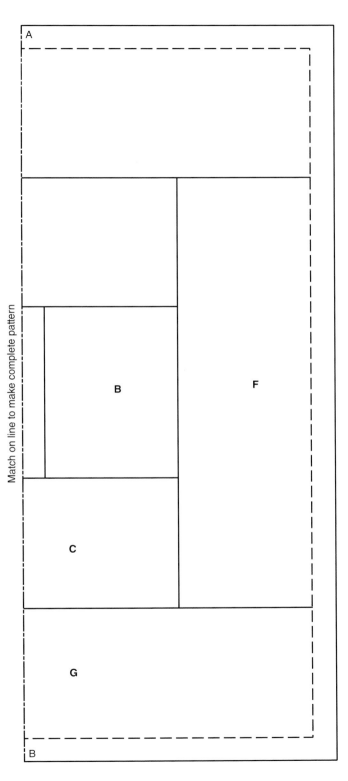

A

Match on line to make complete pattern

B

F

C

G

B

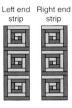

Left end strip   Right end strip

Figure 4

Log blocks to make a left-end strip, again referring to Figure 4. **_Note:_** _Be careful to place the blocks in the proper orientation referring to the Placement Diagram for correct positioning._

4. Sew the right-end strip to the right end and the left-end strip to the left end of the bordered Center Log block to complete the place mat top referring to the Placement Diagram.

5. Remove the paper pieces from all blocks.

6. Press the completed top.

7. Lay the batting rectangle on a flat surface; place the backing right side up on top of the batting. Place the place mat top right sides together with the backing and pin to hold.

8. Sew around edges using a ¼" seam allowance, leaving a 3" opening on one side to turn right side out.

9. Trim batting close to seams and clip corners. Turn right side out through the opening; press edges flat.

10. Turn opening edges to the inside ¼"; hand-stitch opening closed.

11. Quilt as desired by hand or machine.

12. Repeat steps 1–11 to complete the second place mat. ▪

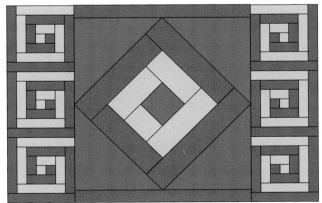

Carved in Stone Place Mat
Placement Diagram 18¹/₂" x 12"

WRAPPED IN ROSES

Stitch a table mat and four matching coasters using a hexagon in the center instead of the traditional square. Fussy-cut the hexagon for an added touch.

DESIGN BY CONNIE KAUFFMAN

PROJECT NOTES

The materials listed are enough to make one table mat and four coasters.

PROJECT SPECIFICATIONS

Skill Level: Advanced
Table Mat Size: 15½" x 14¼"
Coaster Size: 4¼" x 3¾"

MATERIALS

- 9 coordinating fat eighths with one being dark rose
- Batting 16" x 19"
- 4 batting squares 5½" x 5½"
- Backing 16" x 19"
- 4 backing squares 5½" x 5½"
- Neutral-color all-purpose thread
- Quilting thread
- 2 yards ⅜" coordinating corded trim
- Template material
- Basic sewing tools and supplies

CUTTING

1. Prepare template for A using pattern given; cut as directed on the piece. Transfer dots to seam intersections as marked on pattern.

2. Cut the remaining fat eighths into 1½" x 11" strips.

COMPLETING THE TABLE MAT

1. Select six different 1½"-wide strips for first round. Label strips from 1–6.

2. Place strip 1 right sides together on one side of A and stitch from one end of A to the dot on the opposite end as shown in Figure 1; secure stitching at both beginning and end.

Figure 1   **Figure 2**

3. Fold the strip to the right side, press and trim as shown in Figure 2; press seam toward strip.

4. Place strip 2 over A and strip 1 on the right edge, and stitch as shown in Figure 3; press seam toward strip 1.

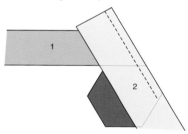

Figure 3

5. Trim strip 2 even with the angle of the A/strip 1 unit as shown in Figure 4.

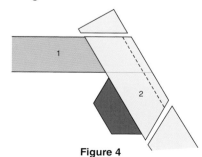

Figure 4

6. Continue adding strips and trimming as in steps 2–5 to complete one round of strips as shown in Figure 5.

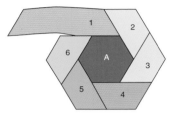

Figure 5

7. Finish partial seam between strip 6 and strip 1 referring to Figure 6. Trim remaining end as shown in Figure 7.

Figure 6

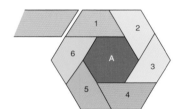

Figure 7

8. Continue adding rounds around the center unit in this manner until you have six rounds to complete the table-mat top.

9. Pin the corded trim around the edges of the table-mat top, easing some fullness at the corners and overlapping at the beginning and end.

10. Using a zipper foot on your machine, machine-baste the trim in place to hold.

11. Place the batting on a flat surface with the backing right side up on top; place the basted table-mat top right sides together with the backing piece. Stitch all around, leaving a 3" opening on one edge.

12. Trim backing and batting even with the edge of the table-mat top; turn right side out through the opening. Turn opening edges ¼" to the inside; hand-stitch opening closed.

13. Quilt as desired by hand or machine to finish.

COMPLETING THE COASTERS

1. Repeat steps 1–6 of Completing the Table Mat to make four coaster tops.

2. Repeat steps 10–12 with one each 5½" x 5½" batting and backing square and coaster top to complete the four coasters. ■

Wrapped in Roses Coaster
Placement Diagram 4¼" x 3¾"

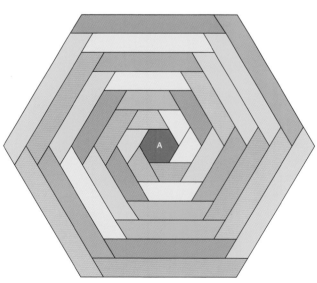

Wrapped in Roses Table Mat
Placement Diagram 15½" x 14¼"

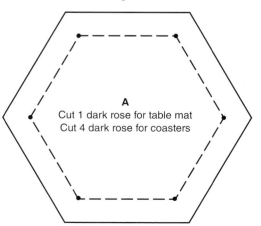

A
Cut 1 dark rose for table mat
Cut 4 dark rose for coasters

LOG CABIN SLOUCHY BAG

Constructed with the quilt-as-you-go method, the inside of this bag is quilted in the same design as the outside.

DESIGN BY CAROL ZENTGRAF

PROJECT NOTES

Turn to page 30 to find instructions and step-by-step photos for the quilt-as-you-go method.

PROJECT SPECIFICATIONS

Skill Level: Beginner
Bag Size: 20" x 20" x 3"
Block Size: 5" x 5"
Number of Blocks: 32

MATERIALS

- ⅝ yard white print
- 1¼ yards brown print
- 1½ yards dark pink print
- Batting 34" x 45"
- Neutral-color all-purpose thread
- 2 (4" x 36") strips fusible interfacing
- Basic sewing tools and supplies

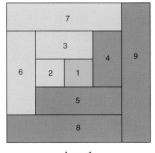

Log 1
5" x 5" Block
Make 8

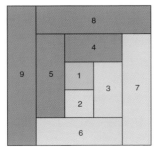

Log 2
5" x 5" Block
Make 8

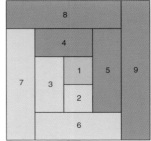

Log 3
5" x 5" Block
Make 8

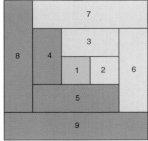

Log 4
5" x 5" Block
Make 8

CUTTING

1. Cut two 7" x 21" strips dark pink print for top band.

2. Cut the remaining dark pink print into 1½" by fabric width strips. Subcut strips into the following for lining:
96–1½" x 1½" squares for Nos. 1 and 2 (32 of these are for No. 1 pieces for block)
64–2½" strips for Nos. 3 and 4
64–3½" strips for Nos. 5 and 6
64–4½" strips for Nos. 7 and 8
32–5½" strips for No. 9

3. Cut (10) 1½" by fabric width strips white print; subcut strips into 32 of each of the following sizes:
1½" x 1½" squares for No. 2
2½" strips for No. 3
3½" strips for No. 6
4½" strips for No. 7

4. Cut two 6" x 36" strips brown print for handles.

5. Cut two 1¼" by fabric width strips brown print for drawstrings.

6. Cut the remaining brown print into (14) 1½" by fabric width strips; subcut strips into 32 of each of the following sizes:
2½" strips for No. 4
3½" strips for No. 5
4½" strips for No. 8
5½" strips for No. 9

7. Cut the batting into 1½" x 45" strips; subcut into the following sizes:
64–1½" x 1½" squares
64–2½" strips
64–3½" strips
64–4½" strips
32–5½" strips

COMPLETING THE BLOCKS

1. To complete one Log 1 block, select one each pieces 1–9 for block and the same-size batting and lining pieces.

2. Referring to Figure 1, layer pieces in this order: No. 2 lining right side up, No. 1 lining wrong side up, No. 1 batting, No. 1 fabric right side up, No. 2 fabric wrong side up and No. 2 batting.

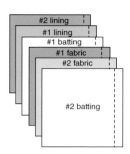

Figure 1

3. Stitch the layers together using a ¼" seam allowance, again referring to Figure 1.

4. Press No. 2 pieces to the right sides with seam between to enclose batting layers in fabric referring to Figure 2.

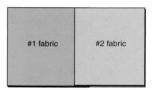

Figure 2

5. Add strip 3 by placing No. 3 lining right sides together with lining side of pieces 1 and 2. Layer right sides together No. 3 fabric with fabric side of pieces 1 and 2, then layer No. 3 batting on top.

6. Stitch the layers together using a ¼" seam allowance.

7. Press No. 3 pieces away from 1 and 2 pieces with seam between to complete the unit as shown in Figure 3.

Figure 3

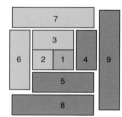

Figure 4

8. Continue adding strips in this manner in a clockwise direction around the center to complete one Log 1 block referring to Figure 4.

9. Repeat steps 1–8, working clockwise when sewing, to complete a total of eight each Log 1 and Log 3 blocks referring to the block drawings for positioning of pieces in the blocks.

10. Working counterclockwise, piece eight each Log 2 and Log 4 blocks referring to the block drawings for positioning of pieces in blocks.

11. Trim all blocks to 5½" x 5½", if necessary.

COMPLETING THE OUTER BAG

1. Lay out the blocks in four rows of four blocks each as shown in Figure 5, paying attention to the design.

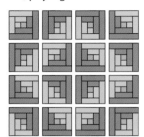

Figure 5

2. Join blocks to make rows; add zigzag-stitch or other edge finish to seam edges to finish. Press seams in adjacent rows in opposite directions.

3. Join the rows to complete the bag front; add zigzag-stitch or other edge finish to seam edges to finish. Press seams in one direction.

4. Repeat steps 1–3 to complete the bag back.

5. With right sides together, sew the bag front and bag back units together along side and bottom edge; finish seam edges as desired.

6. Fold each bottom corner so that the bottom seam is aligned with the side seam as shown in Figure 6; pin.

Figure 6

7. Draw a line across the corner 3" from end point on seams and stitch on the marked line, as shown in Figure 7, to make a box bottom referring to Figure 8.

Figure 7

Figure 8

8. Tack the corner extension to the inside bottom of the bag; turn right side out.

COMPLETING THE BAG

1. Mark a ¾" casing opening ½" above the bottom edge on one long side of each 7" x 21" top-band strip for drawstring as shown in Figure 9.

Figure 9

2. Using a ½" seam allowance, join the two top-band strips on the short ends to make a circular strip, leaving the marked casing openings unstitched as shown in Figure 10; press seams open.

Figure 10

3. Press the opposite long edge of the top band (not the one with the marks for casings) ½" to the wrong side as shown in Figure 11.

Figure 11

4. Pin and stitch the top band to the top edge of the bag with the opening sides right sides together with the bag as shown in Figure 12.

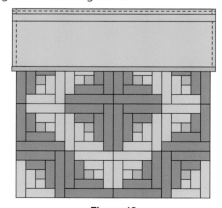

Figure 12

5. Fold the edge with the ½" pressed under to the wrong side and over the seam stitched in step 4; topstitch in place to form the top of the bag as shown in Figure 13.

Figure 13

6. Stitch around the top band ¾" from the bottom seam to make the drawstring casing, again referring to Figure 13.

7. To make each drawstring, press the 1¼" by fabric width strip brown print in half along length with wrong sides together. Open the fold and press the edges to meet at the centerfold as shown in Figure 14; fold in half and press again.

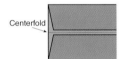

Figure 14   **Figure 15**

8. Stitch the open edges of the strips together to finish the drawings referring to Figure 15.

9. Attach a safety pin to the end of one drawstring. Slide the safety pin and drawstring through one casing opening, through the casing and back out the opposite end, making sure that both ends remain outside the casing when finished as shown in Figure 16.

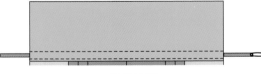

Figure 16

10. Repeat step 9 to insert the remaining drawstring through the opposite casing opening. Remove pin and tie each drawstring end into an overhand knot.

11. To make handles, center and fuse an interfacing strip to the wrong side of each 6" x 36" handle strip.

Repeat steps 7 and 8 to stitch handles, pressing raw ends under ½".

12. Align a handle end inside the bag (with folded ends touching the inside of the bag) 5" away from side seams and ½" below the band stitching and sew in place, referring to Figure 16, to complete the bag. ■

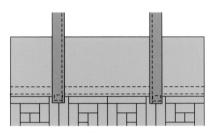

Figure 17

Log Cabin Slouchy Bag
Placement Diagram 20" x 20" x 3"

ORANGE BLOSSOMS AT THE CABIN

Traditional Log Cabin blocks and fusible appliqué make a great over-the-shoulder bag.

DESIGN BY CAROLYN S. VAGTS

PROJECT SPECIFICATIONS

Skill Level: Intermediate
Bag Size: 16" x 14" x 4"
Block Size: 16" x 14"
Number of Blocks: 2

MATERIALS

- Scraps purple and red mottleds or batiks
- ⅛ yard each 5 medium and 5 dark autumn-colored batiks
- 1 fat eighth each orange, yellow and green mottleds or batiks
- 1¾ yards coordinating dark batik for lining, sides, handles and inside pockets
- 1 crib-size batting
- All-purpose thread to match fabrics
- Green all-purpose thread
- ½ yard fusible web
- 2 (1¼") round coordinating buttons
- Water-soluble marker
- 1 gold magnetic snap
- Basic sewing tools and supplies

CUTTING

1. Trace appliqué shapes onto the paper side of the fusible web as directed on patterns for number to cut, leaving space between shapes for cutting.

2. Cut out shapes, leaving a margin around each one.

3. Fuse shapes to the wrong side of fabrics as directed on each piece; cut out shapes on traced lines. Remove paper backing.

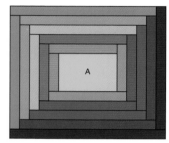

Log Cabin
16" x 14" Block
Make 2

4. Cut two 4½" x 6½" A rectangles yellow mottled or batik.

5. Cut two 1½" by fabric width strips from each ⅛ yard medium and dark batiks.

6. Cut four 14½" x 4½" rectangles for purse and lining side gusset pieces.

7. Cut two 16½" x 14½" rectangles from lining fabric.

8. Cut two 4½" x 16½" rectangles from lining fabric for purse bottom and lining bottom.

9. Cut two 5½" by fabric width strips from lining fabric for handles.

10. Cut one 12½" x 16½" rectangle from lining fabric for inside pockets.

11. Cut two 2" x 40" batting strips from one end of the batting; set aside remainder of batting for purse body, sides and front tabs.

12. Prepare templates for tabs and flap using patterns given; cut as directed on each piece.

COMPLETING THE BLOCKS

1. To complete one Log Cabin block, place the lightest 1½" fabric width strip right sides together on top of a 4½" end of A and stitch as shown in Figure 1.

Figure 1

Figure 2

2. Trim the strip even with A as shown in Figure 2; press the strip to the right side with seam toward the strip.

3. Repeat steps 1 and 2 with the same fabric strip on the top of the stitched A unit referring to Figure 3.

Figure 3

Figure 4

4. Repeat steps 1 and 2 with the lightest dark strip on the opposite 4½" end of A and then on the remaining long edge of A to complete one round of strips on the A rectangle as shown in Figure 4.

5. Continue adding strips around the A rectangle in numerical order, using strips in light to darkest order until you have five lights on two adjacent sides and five darks on the remaining sides to complete one block as shown in Figure 5.

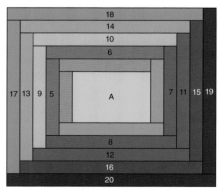

Figure 5

6. Repeat steps 1–5 to complete a second Log Cabin block.

COMPLETING THE OUTER BAG SHELL

1. Using the full-size pattern given and the water-soluble marker, draw the leaf vine onto one completed Log Cabin block referring to Figure 6 and Placement Diagram for positioning.

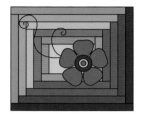

Figure 6

2. Stitch on the marked lines to make leaf stems using green thread.

3. Arrange and fuse a leaf and flower motif in numerical order on the Log Cabin block with the stitched stems, again referring to Figure 6 and Placement Diagram for positioning.

4. Straight-stitch around each fused shape with thread to match fabrics.

5. Join the dark bottom edges of the two Log Cabin blocks with one of the 16½" x 4½" rectangles as shown in Figure 7; press seams open.

Figure 7

Figure 8

6. Sew one of the 14½" x 4½" rectangles with right sides together on each end of the appliquéd Log Cabin block, stopping stitching ¼" from the end of the seam as shown in Figure 8.

7. Lay the stitched outer bag shell pieces right side up on one end of the batting; trim the batting 1" larger all around.

8. Quilt as desired.

9. Place two side tab pieces right sides together on top of a matching batting piece; stitch around three sides, leaving the end open for turning. Trim batting close to stitching; clip corners. Turn right side out; press edges flat. Repeat to make a second side tab and one top flap.

10. If using a magnetic snap closure on the flap, now is the time to install it referring to the manufacturer's instructions. If using a buttonhole and button, now is the time to make the buttonhole in the flap where desired.

11. Fold and press each 5½"-wide handle strip in half lengthwise; unfold. Fold in ½" along one long edge of each 5½"-wide handle strip.

12. Center a 2" x 40" batting strip down the pressed center of each strip and baste through the center to hold in place as shown in Figure 9.

Figure 9   **Figure 10**

13. Fold the long pressed edges over the batting, with pressed edge over raw edge, and stitch in place as shown in Figure 10; remove basting. Topstitch ¼" from each long edge to finish handles. ***Note:*** *You may adjust the length of the handles to a shorter length at this time, if desired.*

14. Join the back and front bag panels with the side strips as in step 6—the bag bottom strip ends will still be loose; press seams to one side.

15. Sew the bottom strip ends to both side panels, stopping stitching ¼" from the ends of each seam.

16. Turn right side out to complete the outer bag shell.

COMPLETING THE BAG

1. Fold the 12½" x 16½" pocket rectangle in half right sides out so it measures 6¼" x 16½"; press.

2. Place the folded pocket rectangle on one of the 16½" x 14½" lining rectangles with the open end at least 4" from the bottom edge of the rectangle; stitch across the open end of the folded pocket rectangle referring to Figure 11. ***Note:*** *The folded pocket section will extend 2¼" beyond the lining piece at the bottom.* Again referring to Figure 11, fold up the pocket rectangle, press flat and pin side edges in place. Measure and mark desired pocket sections. Stitch from top to bottom of the folded pocket to create the pocket sections.

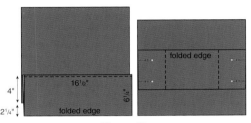

Figure 11

3. Assemble the lining in the same manner as the outer bag shell, except leave a 4" opening in the center of one of the seams when stitching the bottom rectangle to the lining front or back as shown in Figure 12.

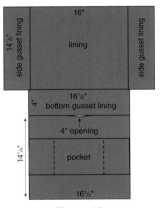

Figure 12

4. Fold the unstitched ends of each side tab under ¼" and press. Position a side tab in place 3" down from the top edge with widest point toward the bottom, and with the straight edge 1" beyond seam between the side and back pieces as shown in Figure 13 on page 104. ***Note:*** *The ¼" turned edge will be enclosed between the outer bag shell and tab.* Stitch a square shape all around the 1" area to secure as shown in Figure 14. Repeat on the opposite side with the second tab.

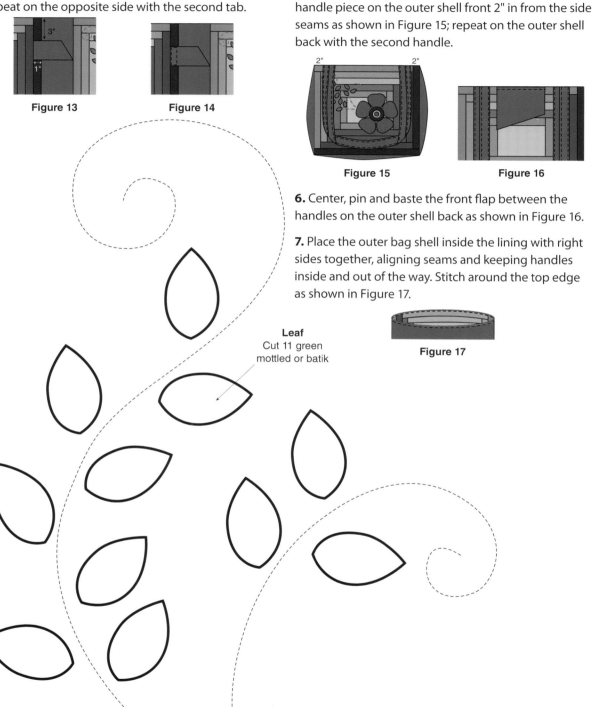

Figure 13

Figure 14

5. Position, pin and machine-baste the ends of one handle piece on the outer shell front 2" in from the side seams as shown in Figure 15; repeat on the outer shell back with the second handle.

Figure 15

Figure 16

6. Center, pin and baste the front flap between the handles on the outer shell back as shown in Figure 16.

7. Place the outer bag shell inside the lining with right sides together, aligning seams and keeping handles inside and out of the way. Stitch around the top edge as shown in Figure 17.

Figure 17

Leaf
Cut 11 green
mottled or batik

Leaf Appliqué Motif

8. Turn right side out through opening left in the bottom of the lining; turn opening edges to the inside and hand- or machine-stitch the opening closed.

9. Press around the top edge; topstitch ¼" from edge.

10. Bring the side tabs around to the front of the purse and attach with the button. ***Note:*** *The tabs should be pulled tight so that it pleats the sides and creates a less-square look. On the sample, the angled end of the tab aligns with one of the fabric strips in the Log Cabin block.* ■

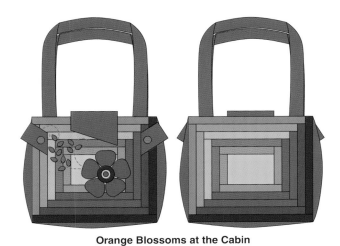

Orange Blossoms at the Cabin
Placement Diagram 16" x 14" x 4"

Petal
Cut 5 orange mottled or batik

Flower Center 3
Cut 1 yellow mottled or batik

Flower Center 2
Cut 1 purple mottled or batik

Flower Center 4
Cut 1 red mottled or batik

Flower Appliqué Motif

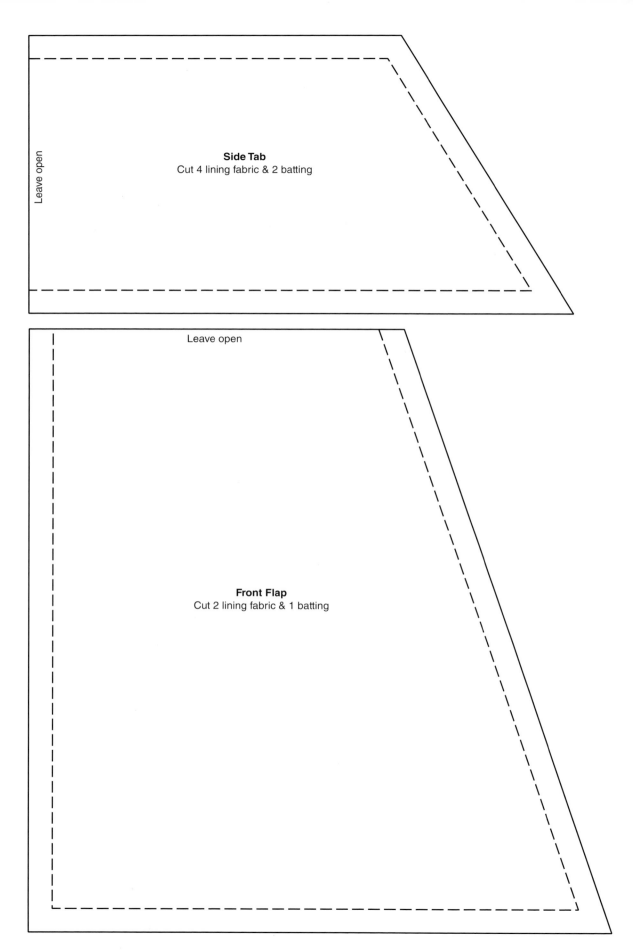

Side Tab
Cut 4 lining fabric & 2 batting

Leave open

Leave open

Front Flap
Cut 2 lining fabric & 1 batting

OVERSIZED QUILT CARRYALL

Create circle appliqués from Log Cabin blocks for a tote bag large enough to carry a king-size bed quilt to your guild meeting for show and tell.

DESIGN BY CHRIS MALONE

PROJECT SPECIFICATIONS

Skill Level: Beginner
Bag Size: 36" x 36" x 4"
Block Size: 7" x 7"
Number of Blocks: 16

MATERIALS

- 12½" x 9½" rectangle black print for inside pocket
- ⅛ yard each 7 assorted color dots
- ⅛ yard each 6 black prints (dots, stripes and florals)
- 2¼ yards black mini dot
- 2½ yards black multicolored dot
- 2 batting squares 39" x 39"
- 2 batting strips 1" x 24"
- All-purpose thread to match fabric
- 1⅔ yards 20"-wide lightweight permanent stabilizer
- 4 (1½"-diameter) cover buttons
- 12" x 18" sheet needlepoint canvas
- Pinking shears (optional)
- Compass
- Basic sewing tools and supplies

CUTTING

1. Cut two 39" x 39" squares black multicolored dots for tote front and back.

2. Cut two 3" x 24" strips black multicolored dots for tote handles.

3. Cut two 39" x 39" squares black mini dot for tote lining.

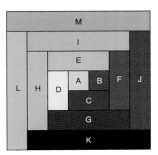

Log Cabin
7" x 7" Block
Make 16

4. From the assorted color dots, cut 1½"-wide strips and subcut into 16 strips each size as follows: 1½" A, 2½" D, 3½" E, 4½" H, 5½" I, 6½" L and 7½" M.

5. From the black prints, cut 1½"-wide strips and subcut into 16 strips each size as follows: 1½" B, 2½" C, 3½" F, 4½" G, 5½"J and 6½" K.

COMPLETING THE BLOCKS & CIRCLE UNITS

1. Select one set of A–M strips to complete one Log Cabin block.

2. Sew B to A; press seam toward B.

3. Continue to add strips to A in alphabetical order, as shown in Figure 1, to complete one Log Cabin block; press seams toward the most recently added strip as they are added except for the M strip. Press the seam of the M strip toward I.

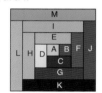

Figure 1

4. Repeat steps 1 and 2 to complete a total of 16 Log Cabin blocks.

5. Arrange and join four Log Cabin blocks into two rows of two blocks each with the black-print sides facing the center of the unit as shown in Figure 2; press seams in opposite directions. Join the rows to complete a four-block unit; press seam in one direction.

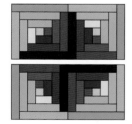

Figure 2

6. Repeat step 5 to complete four four-block units.

7. Using the compass, draw four 14"-diameter circles on the lightweight permanent stabilizer, leaving ½" between shapes; cut apart.

8. Center and pin a stabilizer circle pattern side up on the right side of a four-block unit; sew all around on the line on the stabilizer pattern. Using pinking shears, cut out close to the seam. **Note:** *Using pinking shears eliminates the need to clip curves. If using regular shears, you will need to clip into the curves all around the circle edges.*

9. Cut a 6" slash through the center of the stabilizer only as shown in Figure 3; turn the circle right side out through the opening.

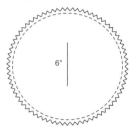

Figure 3

10. Press edges flat to complete one circle unit.

11. Repeat steps 8–10 to complete a total of four circle units.

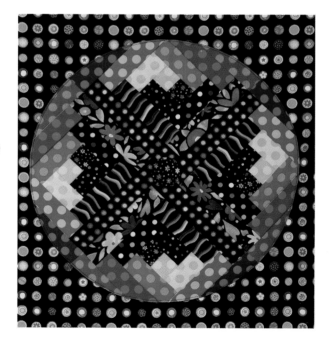

COMPLETING THE OUTER TOTE

1. Arrange the circle units in two rows of two units each on the tote front square, starting the top row 2½" down from the top edge and leaving 4" between the units as shown in Figure 4; pin or baste in place to secure. **Note:** *The units may be placed 90-degrees on point, as shown in the sample, or squared as desired.*

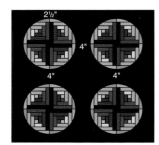

Figure 4

2. Topstitch circle units in place close to the edges.

3. Place and pin the bag front right side up on top of one batting square; repeat with tote back and remaining batting square.

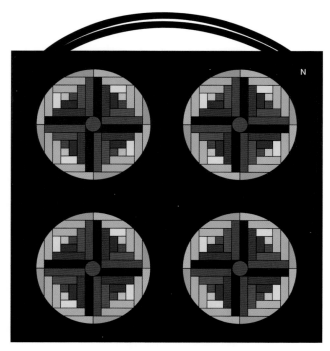

Oversized Quilt Carryall
Placement Diagram 36" x 36" x 4"

4. Mark and cut out a 2½" x 2½" square from each bottom corner of the top front and back pieces as shown in Figure 5.

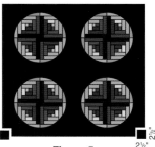

Figure 5

5. Machine-baste tote front and tote back ³⁄₁₆" from the edges.

6. Quilt the tote front and back as desired. **Note:** *The sample is quilted around each circle unit and around the K strips in each circle unit. A 7" circle is quilted in the center. The back repeats the four 14" circles and one 7" circle of quilting.*

7. With right sides together, pin and stitch the tote front to the tote back at the sides and along the bottom as shown in Figure 6; press seams open.

Figure 6

8. To form the bag bottom, match a side seam of one tote side with the bottom seam line and stitch across the resulting straight line as shown in Figure 7. Repeat for the other side seam.

Figure 7

9. To make tote handles, fold and press a ¼" hem to the wrong side along one long side of each 3" x 24" strip.

10. Place a 1" batting strip on the wrong side of each fabric strip ¾" from the raw edge as shown in Figure 8; baste down the center of the batting to hold in place.

Figure 8

11. Fold the raw edge of the fabric strip over the batting, and then fold the hemmed edge on top; pin and press. Edgestitch folded edge and topstitch down both long sides of each strip ³⁄₁₆" from the edge. Remove basting.

12. Align the raw edges on one handle strip at the top of the tote front 5" from side seams and baste in place as shown in Figure 9; repeat with the remaining handle strip on the tote back.

Figure 9

13. Cut two 4" x 8" rectangles from the sheet of needlepoint canvas; butt ends and whipstitch together to make one length as shown in Figure 10.

Figure 10

14. Place the joined needlepoint canvas strip inside at the bottom of the tote, trimming the length if necessary to fit. Tack to the bottom of the tote in a few places to secure.

LINING THE TOTE

1. Fold the 12½" x 9½" black print rectangle in half with right sides together to form a 6¼" x 9½" pocket rectangle as shown in Figure 11; sew all around the three raw sides, leaving a 3" opening on one seam.

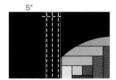

Figure 11

2. Trim corners and turn right side out; press edges flat.

3. Turn opening edges in ¼" and hand-stitch opening closed to complete the pocket.

4. Center and pin the pocket to one of the lining squares 4½" down from the top edge as shown in Figure 12; topstitch close to the edges along sides and bottom.

Figure 12

5. Mark and cut out a 2½" x 2½" square from the bottom corners of the lining front and back pieces.

6. Sew the lining front to the lining back referring to step 7 in Completing the Outer Tote except leave a 6" opening on the bottom seam.

6. Make corners in the lining as in step 8 in Completing the Outer Tote.

7. Place the stitched lining right sides together with the outer tote and align the top edges; stitch all around top edge.

8. Turn right side out through the opening in the tote bottom. Turn opening edges to the inside; hand- or machine-stitch opening closed.

9. Push the lining inside the tote, matching corners. Press top edge flat; topstitch all around top edge.

10. Cover the buttons referring to the product instructions. Hand-stitch a covered button to the center of each circle unit to complete the bag. ■

LACY BIBLE COVER

Combine a paper-pieced Pineapple Log Cabin block, lace, pockets and a button tab for a practical and protective cover for your Bible.

DESIGN BY BARBARA A. CLAYTON

PROJECT NOTE

The lace flowers were cut from packaged lace medallions found in fabric stores with lace collars. If you can't find these in cream or off-white, you can tea dye white lace or use a commercial tan dye to get the desired color. A teaspoon of tan dye in a gallon of warm water was used for the sample. Test the color by dipping a ½" piece of the lace into the dye for 15 seconds; rinse it and let it dry. That combination produced the desired color. All of the lace used was dyed in this manner to make lace to match the cream/tan fabrics used in the blocks.

PROJECT SPECIFICATIONS

Skill Level: Intermediate
Book Cover Size: 17½" x 10½" opened flat
Block Size: 6" x 6"
Number of Blocks: 2

MATERIALS

- 1 fat quarter each 4 different tan/cream tonals
- ½ yard light purple tonal
- ⅝ yard medium purple tonal
- ⅔ yard dark purple tonal
- 24" x 45" rectangle batting
- Neutral-color all-purpose thread
- Purple and cream quilting thread
- Clear .004 nylon thread
- 2 (¾") round buttons
- ¼ yard ½"-wide upholstery trim
- ⅔ yard ⅝"-wide cream floral lace
- 2 (1⅝" x 2½") lace flowers
- Pencil or white chalk
- Basic sewing tools and supplies

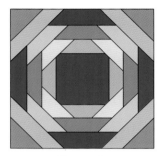

Pineapple
6" x 6" Block
Make 2

CUTTING

1. Cut one 3½" by fabric width strip dark purple tonal; subcut strip into one 6½" A rectangle and two 2¾" x 2¾" squares for piece 1. Cut the remainder of the strip into 1¼"-wide strips for pieces 18–21.

2. Cut one 11" x 18" D rectangle dark purple tonal.

3. Cut 1¾" bias strips from the remainder of the dark purple tonal to total 200" when joined to make one long strip.

4. Cut one 6½" by fabric width strip medium purple tonal; subcut strip into two 1¾" x 6½" B strips and two 2¾" x 18" C strips.

5. Cut one 5½" by fabric width strip medium purple tonal; subcut strip into two 7¼" F rectangles and four 1¾" x 11½" J handle strips.

6. Cut two 1¼" by fabric width strips medium purple tonal for pieces 10–13.

7. Cut one 11" by fabric width strip light purple tonal; subcut strip into four 7¼" E rectangles and four 2½" x 1½" strips for pieces 2–5.

8. Assign a number to each of the four cream/tan tonals. Cut 1¼" by fabric width strips from each cream/tan tonal 1, 2 and 3 for pieces 6–9 (No. 1), 14–17 (No. 2) and 22–25 (No. 3).

9. Cut 1½" by fabric width strips cream/tan tonal No. 4 for pieces 26–29.

10. Prepare templates using patterns given; cut as directed on each piece.

11. Cut one 20" x 13" and two 11" x 7¼" rectangles, one 5½" x 7¼" rectangle and two 1¾" x 11½" strips batting.

COMPLETING THE PINEAPPLE BLOCKS

1. Make two copies of the Pineapple paper-piecing pattern using the pattern given.

2. To complete one Log Cabin block, pin piece 1 square to the center of the unmarked side of the paper pattern as shown in Figure 1. ***Note:*** *Hold the paper pattern up to a window or on a light table to align the square in the right position.*

Figure 1

3. Measure the length of piece 2 on the pattern and add ¼" to the measurement; cut a light purple tonal piece from the previously cut 1¼"-wide strips that size or slightly longer.

4. Place and pin piece 2 right side down on top of piece 1 with the edge of piece 2 even with the edge of piece 1 as shown in Figure 2.

Figure 2

5. Set your machine to a very close stitch (18–20 stitches per inch) so that the paper will tear away from the sewing line easier later.

6. Turn the paper over and sew along the line between pieces 1 and 2, beginning sewing ¼" from the line and ending ¼" past the line as shown in Figure 3.

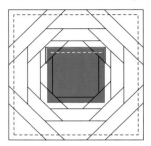

Figure 3

7. Turn the paper over to the fabric side and fold piece 2 to the right side and press flat; pin to hold in place.

8. Select piece 3 according to the pattern. Lay right side down on top of pieces 1 and 2 with the edge of the piece even with the edges of pieces 1 and 2.

9. Turn the pattern over and sew on the line between pieces 1, 2 and 3. Flip the fabric back, press and trim as in step 7; trim excess of piece 2 to reduce bulk before adding piece 4 as shown in Figure 4.

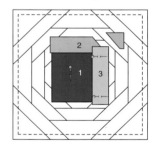

Figure 4

10. Continue adding pieces in numerical and color order referring to the paper-piecing pattern to complete one Pineapple block.

11. Repeat steps 2–10 to complete a total of two Pineapple blocks.

12. Remove paper from the back side of the blocks.

COMPLETING THE OUTER COVER

1. Sew a Pineapple block to each long side of the dark purple tonal A; press seams toward A.

2. Sew a B strip to opposite short ends and C strips to the long sides of the A/block unit to complete the pieced outer cover; press seams toward B and C strips.

3. Using the pencil or white chalk, draw vertical quilting lines 1" apart on the B and C pieces and diagonal grid lines 1" apart on A as shown in Figure 5.

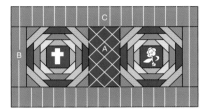

Figure 5

4. Sandwich a 20" x 13" batting rectangle between the pieced outer cover and the D rectangle; pin or baste to hold layers together.

5. Using white quilting thread, quilt on the marked lines on A. Using purple quilting thread, quilt on the marked lines on B and C.

6. Machine-quilt in the ditch of Pineapple block seam using the .004 clear nylon thread.

7. When quilting is complete, trim batting even with the edges of D and the pieced outer cover.

8. Pin a large lace flower to the center square in the front-side Pineapple block; hand-stitch in place.

9. To make a lace cross, cut a 2½" and a 2" strip from the upholstery trim; turn the ends of each strip under ¼".

10. Center the longer strip on the center square in the back-side Pineapple block; hand-stitch in place. Place the remaining shorter strip across the first strip to form a cross ½" from the top edge of the stitched strip as shown in Figure 6; hand-stitch in place.

Figure 6

11. Pin and hand-stitch the lace yardage close to the seam all around the center block unit referring to the project photo and Placement Diagram to complete the outer cover.

COMPLETING THE FRONT INSIDE FLAP

1. Center and pin another large lace flower 1½" down from one 7¼" edge of one E rectangle; hand-stitch in place.

2. Draw vertical quilting lines 1" apart on the same E rectangle and one remaining E rectangle. Draw a diagonal grid 1" apart in both directions on the 5½" x 7¼" F rectangle using the pencil or white chalk.

3. Sandwich matching size batting rectangles between the marked E and F rectangles and the same-size lining pieces. Hand-quilt on the marked lines and an outline around the lace flower using purple quilting thread. Set aside the quilted E rectangle without the lace flower for back inside flap.

4. Pin and stitch the prepared bias strip right sides together on the top edge of the quilted F pocket as shown in Figure 7; trim excess bias. Fold under ¼" on the unstitched long edge and press; fold the strip to the wrong side of F and machine- or hand-stitch in place on the lining side of F.

Figure 7

5. Pin and stitch a length of lace yardage just below the binding on the F pocket.

6. Pin the F pocket to the bottom half of the quilted E rectangle; finish the right-side long edge with the bias strip as in step 4 to complete the front inside flap as shown in Figure 8. Machine-stitch close to the remaining edges to hold flat.

Figure 8

COMPLETING THE BACK INSIDE FLAP

1. Draw diagonal quilting lines 1" apart on the dark purple tonal H pocket piece; sandwich the same-size batting between the marked H and the lining H. Quilt on the marked lines using dark purple quilting thread.

2. Bind the curved edges and then the top edge of the H pocket using the bias strip as in step 4 of Completing the Front Inside Flap.

3. Sandwich the G batting, top and lining pieces; pin layers together and bind curved edges and then the top edge using bias strip referring to step 4 of Completing the Front Inside Flap, turning ends in at both ends to form the G flap. Hand-quilt ¼" away from the curved edges.

4. Hand-stitch a length of lace yardage to the top edge just below the binding.

5. Center and machine-stitch a ¾" buttonhole on the G flap about ⅝" up from the bottom edge; cut the buttonhole open in the center to accommodate the button.

6. Center and stitch the two sides and bottom edge of the H bottom pocket in the ditch of the bias seam onto the quilted E rectangle 2¼" up from the bottom edge as shown in Figure 9.

Figure 9

7. Hand-stitch the outer bias edge of the H pocket in place around sides and bottom edges.

8. Center the top G flap over the H pocket about 2¼" down from the top edge of E and stitch top edge in place as in steps 6 and 7.

9. Center and sew a button on the H pocket to fit into the previously stitched buttonhole on the G flap.

10. Finish the left-side long edge with the bias strip as in step 4 of Completing the Front Inside Flap and machine-stitch close to edges on the remaining sides to complete the back inside flap as shown in Figure 10.

Figure 10

COMPLETING THE LACY BIBLE COVER

1. Place the completed front and back inside flaps on the D side of the completed front cover, matching raw edges as shown in Figure 11; machine-baste in place close to the edges to hold.

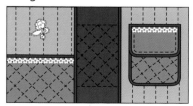

Figure 11

2. Sandwich a same-size batting piece between two J pieces; bind curved edges as in step 4 of Completing the Front Inside Flap. Hand-quilt ¼" from binding using purple quilting thread. Repeat for second set of J handle pieces.

3. Repeat step 2 with the I tab pieces.

4. Machine-stitch a ¾" buttonhole ¼" in from the center of the curved end of the quilted I piece as shown in Figure 12.

Figure 12

5. Center and pin the raw edge of I to the raw edge of one end of the back inside flap end of the stitched unit as shown in Figure 13.

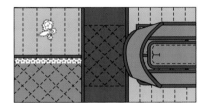

Figure 13

6. Pin one end of each J handle ⅛" from the sides of the centered I tab, again referring to Figure 13; baste to hold in place.

7. Repeat step 6 with J on the opposite end of the front inside flap end of the stitched unit leaving space between the J ends to match the spacing at the opposite end as shown in Figure 14.

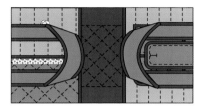

Figure 14

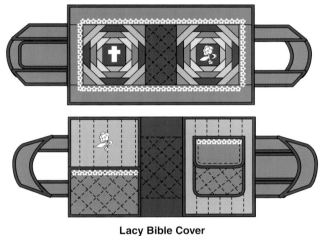

Lacy Bible Cover
Placement Diagram 17½" x 10½" opened flat

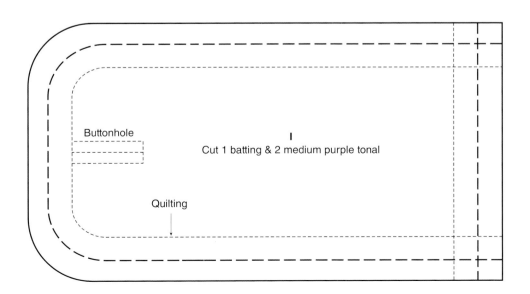

Buttonhole

I
Cut 1 batting & 2 medium purple tonal

Quilting

8. Bind all around outer edge of the layered unit referring to step 4 of Completing the Front Inside Flap, mitering corners and overlapping at the beginning and end.

9. Pull the I tab and J handles to their outward positions and slipstitch to the outer edge of the bias binding to hold open and flat to finish.

10. Insert your book or Bible into the inside flaps. Pull the I button flap over and mark where the button should be. Sew the remaining ¾" button on the outside edge of the book cover where marked to finish. ■

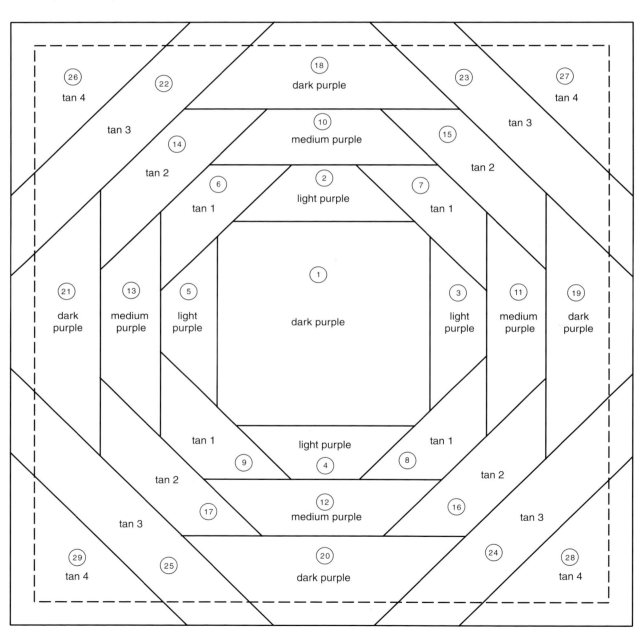

Pineapple Paper-Piecing Pattern
Make 2 copies

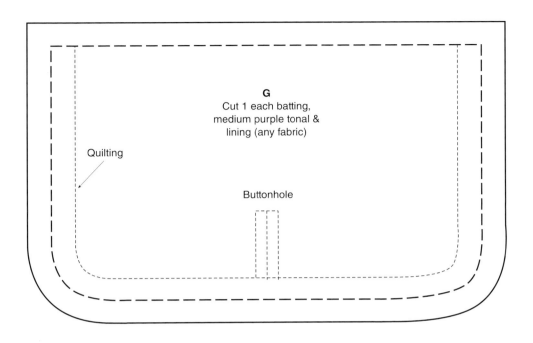

G
Cut 1 each batting,
medium purple tonal &
lining (any fabric)

Quilting

Buttonhole

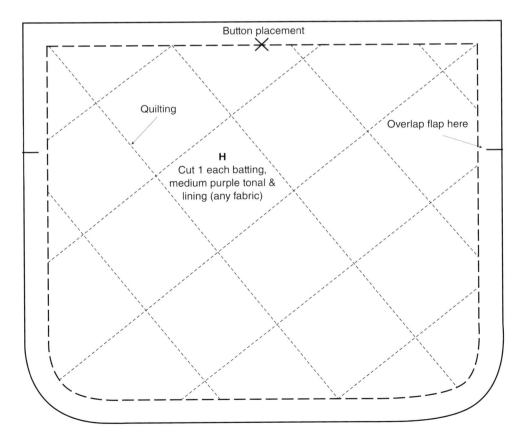

Button placement

Quilting

Overlap flap here

H
Cut 1 each batting,
medium purple tonal &
lining (any fabric)

WHO'S AT THE ZOO?

Using panels framed with Log Cabin strips gives you a head start on this baby quilt. It's super quick and easy.

DESIGN BY CHRIS MALONE

PROJECT SPECIFICATIONS

Skill Level: Beginner
Quilt Size: 46½" x 46½"
Block Size: 13½" x 13½"
Number of Blocks: 9

MATERIALS

- 1 printed quilt panel cut into (9) 8" x 8" squares
- ⅛ yard each 12–14 assorted prints to coordinate with the printed panel
- ½ yard coordinating stripe
- ⅝ yard cream print
- Batting 55" x 55"
- Backing 55" x 55"
- Neutral-color all-purpose thread
- Quilting thread
- 24" length medium rickrack in green, brown and blue, or coordinating colors
- Coordinating colors No. 8 pearl cotton
- Basic sewing tools and supplies

CUTTING

1. Cut printed quilt panel into nine 8" x 8" squares.

2. Cut nine strips each of the following sizes from the assorted prints:
9–2" x 17½"; subcut each strip into one each 8" A and 9½" B strips.
9–2" x 20½"; subcut each strip into one each 9½" C and 11" D strips.
9–2" x 23½"; subcut each strip into one each 11" E and 12½" F strips.
9–2" x 26½"; subcut each strip into one each 12½" G and 14" H.

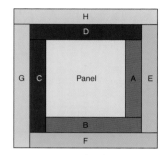

Log Cabin
13½" x 13½" Block
Make 9

3. Cut (16) 2" x 2" J sashing squares total from the assorted prints.

4. Cut eight 2" by fabric width strips cream print; subcut strips into (24) 14" I sashing strips.

5. Cut five 2¼" by fabric width strips coordinating stripe for binding.

COMPLETING THE BLOCKS

1. Cut the three pieces of rickrack into nine 8" lengths. Baste one length of rickrack along one long edge of each printed panel.

2. To complete one Log Cabin block, select one printed panel and one set of A–H strips, selecting matching A/B, C/D, E/F and G/H strips.

3. Referring to Figure 1, sew the A strip to the right side edge and the B strip to the bottom of the printed panel; press seams toward A and B strips. ***Note:*** *The printed panels are directional, so it is important to sew all blocks with the A strip in the same place on the blocks.*

Figure 1

1. Select and join three Log Cabin blocks with four I sashing strips to make a block row referring to Figure 3; press seams toward I strips. Repeat to make three block rows.

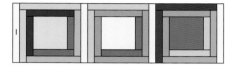

Figure 3

2. Join three I sashing strips with four J sashing squares to make a sashing row referring to Figure 4; press seams toward I strips. Repeat to make four sashing rows.

Figure 4

3. Join the block rows with the sashing rows, beginning and ending with a sashing row, to complete the quilt top; press seams toward sashing rows.

4. Layer, quilt and bind referring to Finishing Your Quilt on page 175.

5. Embellish each printed panel using assorted colors of pearl cotton and a running stitch or French knots. *Note: An example of embellishment stitches are the French knots in the center of some of the owls' eyes and outline stitching close to the edge of the elephant's body.* ▪

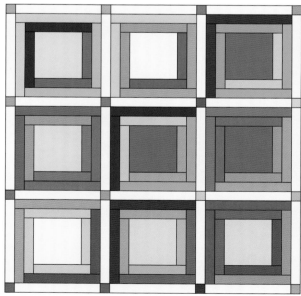

Who's at the Zoo
Placement Diagram 46½" x 46½"

4. Continue to add the strips to the printed panel in alphabetical order to complete one Log Cabin block referring to Figure 2; press seams toward strips as added.

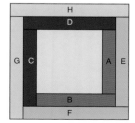

Figure 2

5. Repeat steps 2–4 to complete a total of nine Log Cabin blocks.

BLISSFUL IN THE CLOUDS

Creating kites with Log Cabin blocks and rickrack makes a fun wall quilt for a child's room.

DESIGN BY WENDY SHEPPARD

PROJECT SPECIFICATIONS

Skill Level: Advanced Beginner
Quilt Size: 32" x 50"
Block Sizes: 6" x 6" and 6" x 10"
Number of Blocks: 4 and 4

MATERIALS

- ¼ yard orange print
- ⅓ yard medium blue mottled
- ⅓ yard blue print
- ⅓ yard multicolored print
- ½ yard light blue mottled
- ⅝ yard white mottled
- 1⅜ yard green print
- Batting 40" x 58"
- Backing 40" x 58"
- Neutral-color all-purpose thread
- 1¼ yards multicolored rickrack
- 1 yard ¾"-wide purple-with-white-dots grosgrain ribbon
- Basic sewing tools and supplies

CUTTING

Note: *Sorting all pieces into groups for each block will make choosing the appropriate piece to sew easier.*

1. Cut one 6½" by fabric width strip medium blue mottled; subcut strip into three 10½" G rectangles.

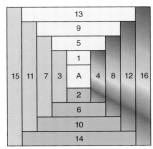

Courthouse Steps
6" x 6" Block
Make 4

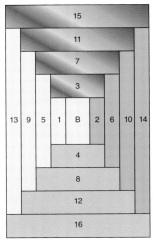

Elongated Courthouse Steps A
6" x 10" Block
Make 2

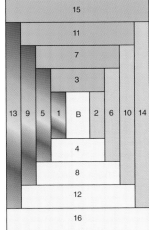

Elongated Courthouse Steps B
6" x 10" Block
Make 2

2. Cut one 6½" by fabric width strip light blue mottled; subcut strip into two 6½" D squares, one 10½" E rectangle, four 1½" x 1½" A squares and four 1½" x 2½" B rectangles.

3. Cut two 1⅛" by fabric width strips light blue mottled. Subcut strips into four each of the following sizes for the Courthouse Steps blocks: 1½" (No. 1), 2¾" (No. 5), 4" (No. 9) and 5¼" (No 13).

4. Cut two 1⅛" by fabric width strips light blue mottled. Subcut strips into two each of the following sizes for the Elongated Courthouse Steps A blocks: 2½" (No. 1), 4½" (No. 5), 6½" (No. 9) and 8½" (No. 13).

5. Cut one 1½" by fabric width strips light blue mottled. Subcut strips into two each of the following sizes for the Elongated Courthouse Steps B blocks: 2¾" (No. 4), 4" (No. 8), 5¼" (No. 12) and 6½" (No. 16).

6. Cut two 6½" by fabric width strips white mottled; subcut strips into two 6½" C squares, four 10½" F rectangles and two 1½" x 26½" I strips.

7. Cut two 1½" x 42½" H strips white mottled.

8. Cut two 1⅛" by fabric width strips orange print. Subcut strips into four each of the following for the Courthouse Steps blocks: 1½" (No. 2), 2¾" (No. 6), 4" (No. 10) and 5¼" (No. 14).

9. Cut two 1⅛" by fabric width strips orange print. Subcut strips into two each of the following sizes for the Elongated Courthouse Steps A blocks: 2½" (No. 2), 4½" (No. 6), 6½" (No. 10) and 8½" (No. 14).

10. Cut one 1½" by fabric width strips orange print. Subcut strips into two each of the following sizes for the Elongated Courthouse Steps B blocks: 2¾" (No. 3), 4" (No. 7), 5¼" (No. 11) and 6½" (No. 15).

11. Cut two 1⅛" by fabric width strips multicolored print. Subcut strips into four each of the following sizes for the Courthouse Steps blocks: 2¾" (No. 4), 4" (No. 8), 5¼" (No. 12) and 6½" (No. 16).

12. Cut two 1½" by fabric width strips multicolored print. Subcut strips into two each of the following sizes for the Elongated Courthouse Steps A blocks: 2¾" (No. 3), 4" (No. 7), 5¼" (No. 11) and 6½" (No 15).

13. Cut two 1⅛" by fabric width strips multicolored print. Subcut strips into two each of the following sizes for the Elongated Courthouse Steps B blocks: 2½" (No. 1), 4½" (No. 5), 6½" (No. 9) and 8½" (No. 13).

14. Cut two 1⅛" by fabric width strips blue print. Subcut strips into four each of the following for the Courthouse Steps blocks: 2¾" (No. 3), 4" (No. 7), 5¼" (No. 11) and 6½" (No. 15).

15. Cut two 1½" by fabric width strips blue print. Subcut strips into two each of the following sizes for the Elongated Courthouse Steps A blocks: 2¾" (No. 4), 4" (No. 8), 5¼" (No. 12) and 6½" (No. 16).

16. Cut two 1⅛" by fabric width strips blue print. Subcut strips into four each of the following sizes for the Elongated Courthouse Steps B blocks: 2½" (No. 2), 4½" (No. 6), 6½" (No. 10) and 8½" (No. 14).

17. Cut two 3½" x 44½" J strips and two 3½" x 32½" K strips along the length of the green print.

18. Cut four 2¼"-wide binding strips along the length of the remaining width of the green print.

COMPLETING THE COURTHOUSE STEPS BLOCKS

1. Referring to Figure 1, sew a 1⅛" x 1½" No. 1 piece to one side and a 1½" x 1⅛" No. 2 piece to opposite sides of A; press seams toward pieces 1 and 2.

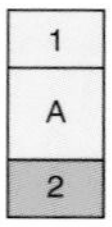

Figure 1

2. Continue adding pieces to opposite sides of A in numerical order until you have four strips on each side of A to complete one Courthouse Steps block as shown in Figure 2; press seams toward strips as added.

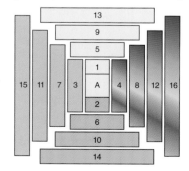

Figure 2

3. Repeat steps 1 and 2 to complete a total of four Courthouse Steps blocks.

COMPLETING THE ELONGATED COURTHOUSE STEPS BLOCKS

1. Sew 1⅛" x 2½" No. 1 light blue mottled piece to one side and a 1⅛" x 2½" No. 2 orange print piece to the opposite side of B as shown in Figure 3; press seams toward pieces 1 and 2.

Figure 3

2. Continue adding pieces to opposite sides of B in numerical order until you have four 1⅛"-wide light blue mottled and orange print strips on two opposite long sides and four 1½"-wide blue print and multicolored print strips on the opposite short sides of B to complete one Elongated Courthouse Steps A block as shown in Figure 4; press seams toward strips as added. Repeat to make a second A block.

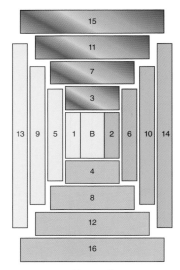

Figure 4

3. Sew 1⅛" x 2½" No. 1 multicolored print piece to one side and a 1⅛" x 2½" No. 2 blue print piece to the opposite side of B as shown in Figure 5; press seams toward pieces 1 and 2.

Figure 5

4. Continue adding pieces to opposite sides of B in numerical order until you have four 1⅛"-wide multicolored print and blue print strips on two opposite long sides and four 1½"-wide light blue mottled and orange print strips on the opposite short sides of B to complete one Elongated Courthouse Steps B block as shown in Figure 6; press seams toward strips as added. Repeat to make a second B block.

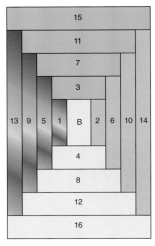

Figure 6

COMPLETING THE QUILT

1. Select two Courthouse Steps blocks; join to make a row as shown in Figure 7. Press seam to one side.

2. Select one each Elongated Courthouse Steps A and B blocks; join to make a row, again referring to Figure 7. Press seam to one side.

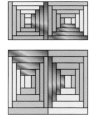

Figure 7

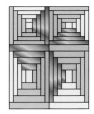

Figure 8

3. Join the two rows to complete a Kite unit as shown in Figure 8; press seam to one side.

4. Repeat steps 1–3 to complete two kite units.

5. Sew a C square to a D square and an F rectangle to an E rectangle as shown in Figure 9; press seams toward D and E. Join the two units to complete a C-D-E-F rectangle unit, again referring to Figure 9; press seams to one side.

Figure 9

6. Sew a D square to a C square and G rectangle to an F rectangle as shown in Figure 10. Join the two units to complete a C-D-G-F rectangle unit, again referring to Figure 10.

Figure 10

7. Sew the C-D-E-F rectangle unit to one kite unit and the C-D-G-F rectangle unit to the remaining kite unit to make rows as shown in Figure 11; press seams away from the kite units.

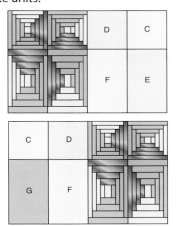

Figure 11

8. Join the two kite units referring to the Placement Diagram for positioning; press seam to one side.

9. Join the two remaining F and G rectangles to make an F/G row as shown in Figure 12; press seams toward G.

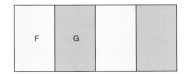

Figure 12

10. Sew the F/G row to the joined kite units to complete the pieced center; press seam toward the F/G row.

11. Sew an H strip to opposite long sides and I strips to the top and bottom of the pieced center; press seams toward H and I strips.

12. Sew J strips to opposite long sides and K strips to the top and bottom of the pieced center; press seams toward J and K strips to complete the pieced top.

13. Layer, quilt and bind referring to Finishing Your Quilt on page 175.

14. Cut one 25" length and one 14" length of multicolored rickrack for kite tails.

15. Arrange the rickrack below each kite unit, starting in the center bottom of each unit and angling at a pleasing gentle curve; stitch in place.

16. Cut the grosgrain ribbon into two equal-length pieces. Tie into a bow. Place the bow at the bottom center on top of the rickrack and securely hand-stitch in place to finish. ▪

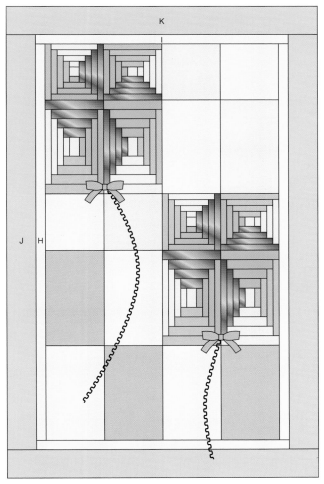

Blissful in the Clouds
Placement Diagram 32" x 50"

LOTS OF DOTS BABY BLOCKS

Easy appliqué on a muslin foundation creates three fun, whimsical blocks just right for Baby.

DESIGN BY CAROL ZENTGRAF

PROJECT SPECIFICATIONS

Skill Level: Beginner
Project Block Size: 4" x 4" x 4"
Block Size: 4" x 4"
Number of Blocks: 12

MATERIALS FOR SET OF 3 BLOCKS

- Scraps black, tan, red, brown, green, pink, yellow and blue
- ⅛ yard white solid
- 1 fat quarter each 6–8 stripe and dot fabrics
- ⅜ yard muslin
- All-purpose thread to match fabrics
- ¼ yard fusible web
- 1 black fine-point permanent fabric pen
- Polyester fiberfill
- Basic sewing tools and supplies

CUTTING

1. Cut two 4½" by fabric width strips muslin; subcut strips into (12) 4½" foundation squares.

2. Cut one 3" by fabric width strip white solid; subcut strip into (12) 3" A squares.

3. Cut six 4½" x 4½" B squares total from the stripe and dot fabrics.

4. Trace appliqué shapes onto the paper side of the fusible web as directed on each pattern for number to cut, leaving at least ¼" between shapes.

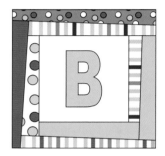

Appliquéd Log Cabin
4" x 4" Block
Make 12

5. Cut out shapes, leaving a margin around each one. Fuse shapes to the wrong side of the fabric scraps and stripe and dot fabrics as directed on patterns for color. Cut out shapes on traced lines; remove paper backing.

6. Cut 1"-wide strips across the remaining width of the stripe and dot fabrics.

COMPLETING THE APPLIQUÉ

1. To complete one Log Cabin block, select an appliqué shape or motif; center and fuse to an A square in numerical order, if there are several pieces in the motif.

2. Using coordinating thread and a narrow zigzag stitch, sew around each of the larger shapes. *Note: The eyes and noses on the dog and bear may be too small to stitch. They may be drawn on as in the next step.*

3. Add facial details to the dog and bear using the black fine-point permanent fabric pen.

COMPLETING THE LOG CABIN BLOCKS

1. To complete one Appliquéd Log Cabin block, center an appliquéd A square on a muslin square as shown in Figure 1; baste to hold in place.

Figure 1   **Figure 2**

2. Select a dot or stripe strip for strip 1; place the strip right sides together on one side of A and stitch, starting and ending stitching at the edge of A referring to Figure 2.

3. Trim strip 1 somewhat even with the A square and press to the right side as shown in Figure 3.

Figure 3   **Figure 4**

4. Trim strip 1 to make a slightly uneven, angled strip as shown in Figure 4.

5. Continue to add strips around A, trimming, pressing and trimming the strips at an angle, until the foundation square is completely covered as shown in Figure 5.

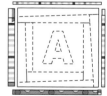

Figure 5   **Figure 6**

6. Trim excess strips even with the foundation square as shown in Figure 6 to complete one block.

7. Repeat steps 1–6 to complete a total of 12 Appliquéd Log Cabin blocks.

COMPLETING THE TOY BLOCKS

1. To complete one toy block, select the Appliquéd Log Cabin blocks with the letters A and B and the apple blocks and the apple and bear blocks; join to make a block strip, alternating motifs with letters and beginning and ending stitching ¼" from the edges of the blocks as shown in Figure 7; press seams in one direction.

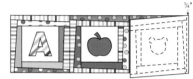

Figure 7

2. Join the ends of the strip to make a tube, beginning and ending stitching ¼" from the edges as shown in Figure 8; press seam to one side.

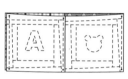

Figure 8   **Figure 9**

3. With right sides together, sew a B square to the stitched tube, starting and stopping stitching ¼" from edge as shown in Figure 9.

4. Repeat step 3 with a second B square, leaving part of one side open.

5. Turn right side out through the opening; press opening edges to the inside ¼".

6. Stuff with fiberfill through the opening; when satisfied with fullness, hand-stitch the opening closed to finish one block.

7. Repeat steps 1–6 with the C and D letters and dog and cherry Appliquéd Log Cabin blocks to make a second toy block.

8. Repeat steps 1–6 with the E and F letters and the flower and egg Appliquéd Log Cabin blocks to make a third toy block. ◼

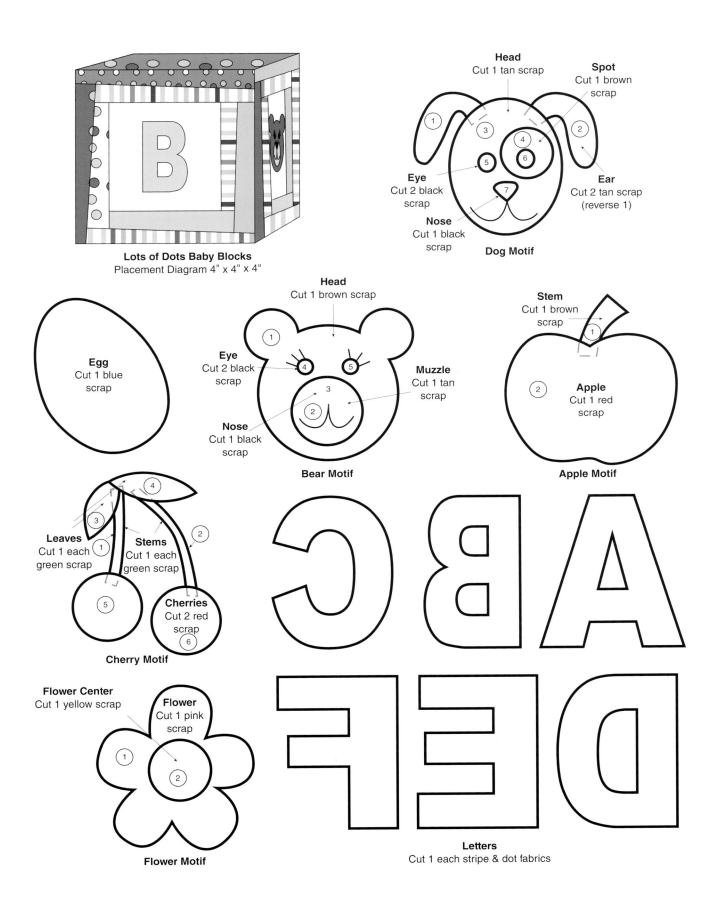

Lots of Dots Baby Blocks
Placement Diagram 4" x 4" x 4"

Head
Cut 1 tan scrap

Spot
Cut 1 brown scrap

Eye
Cut 2 black scrap

Nose
Cut 1 black scrap

Ear
Cut 2 tan scrap (reverse 1)

Dog Motif

Egg
Cut 1 blue scrap

Head
Cut 1 brown scrap

Eye
Cut 2 black scrap

Nose
Cut 1 black scrap

Muzzle
Cut 1 tan scrap

Bear Motif

Stem
Cut 1 brown scrap

Apple
Cut 1 red scrap

Apple Motif

Leaves
Cut 1 each green scrap

Stems
Cut 1 each green scrap

Cherries
Cut 2 red scrap

Cherry Motif

Flower Center
Cut 1 yellow scrap

Flower
Cut 1 pink scrap

Flower Motif

Letters
Cut 1 each stripe & dot fabrics

STRIPES & DOTS BABY BIB

Start with a small appliqué motif in the middle of a fabric foundation and add Log Cabin strips to create this fun bib for Baby.

DESIGN BY CAROL ZENTGRAF

PROJECT SPECIFICATIONS

Skill Level: Beginner
Bib Size: 12½" x 8½"

MATERIALS

- Scraps yellow and pink fabrics
- 9" x 12" rectangle muslin for foundation
- 3" x 3" square white solid
- 1"–1½"-wide strips of assorted stripe and dot fabrics in varying lengths
- ½ yard dot fabric for backing, binding and strips
- All-purpose thread to match binding
- Scrap fusible web
- Sew-on snap
- Basic sewing tools and supplies

CUTTING

1. Prepare bib pattern given on page 134 and trace onto paper to make a full-size pattern; cut as directed on pattern.

2. Cut a 2" x 15" bias strip from the dot fabric for inside neck binding.

3. Cut and piece a 2" x 36" bias strip from the dot fabric to bind outer edges of the bib.

4. Trace appliqué shapes onto the paper side of the scrap of fusible web as directed on pattern; cut out shapes, leaving a margin around each one.

5. Fuse shapes to the wrong side of the pink and yellow scraps as directed on patterns. Cut out shapes on traced lines; remove paper backing.

COMPLETING THE BIB

1. Center the flower motif on the 3" x 3" square white solid; fuse in place.

2. Center the fused square on the muslin bib foundation as shown in Figure 1; baste to hold in place. Using a narrow zigzag-stitch, sew around shapes using thread to match binding. ***Note:*** *Refer to Free-Form Foundation Piecing on Muslin on page 24 for more information about foundation piecing Log Cabins.*

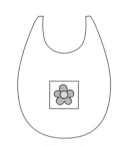

Figure 1

3. Cut a strip of fabric from the 1"–1½"-wide assorted strips at least as long as the appliquéd center square that was pinned to the foundation square.

4. Place this strip right side down on the starting square and sew through all layers—strip, square and muslin. Flip the strip to the right side and press flat; trim ends even with the square as shown in Figure 2. Trim strip at a slight angle, again referring to Figure 2.

Figure 2

5. Sew another strip to the next side, making sure the strip is at least as long as the side you are covering. Flip this strip to the right side, press flat and trim even with the square, if necessary. Trim strip at a slight angle.

6. Continue to add strips round and round, trimming strips at slight angles, until you have covered the muslin bib foundation. Press the stitched unit.

7. Trim the excess strips to conform to the shape of the muslin bib foundation as shown in Figure 3.

Figure 3

8. Place the bib front right side up on the wrong side of the bib backing; baste edges.

9. Press the 2" x 15" binding strip in half along length with wrong sides together. Open the strip; press both long edges to the wrong side to meet the center as shown in Figure 4.

Figure 4

10. Wrap the binding around the neck edge, enclosing the layered bib and edgestitch in place as shown in Figure 5.

Figure 5

11. Repeat step 9 with the 2" x 36" strip of bias binding. Unfold strip and press short ends to the wrong side; refold, enclosing ends. Beginning 2" from one end of the binding strip, wrap the binding around the outer edges of the bib and edgestitch in place as in step 10, continuing the stitching along the extended ends as shown in Figure 6.

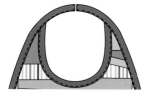

Figure 6

12. Sew the snap halves to the ends of the binding to finish. ■

Stripes & Dots Baby Bib
Placement Diagram 12½" x 8½"

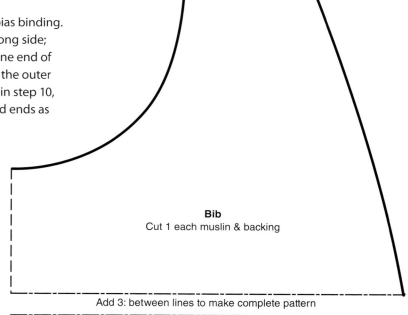

Bib
Cut 1 each muslin & backing

Add 3: between lines to make complete pattern

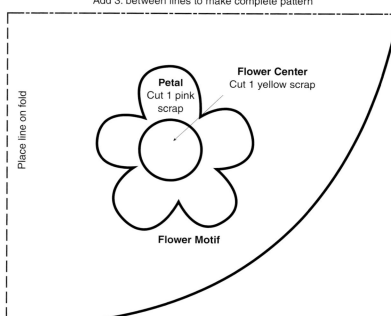

Place line on fold

Petal
Cut 1 pink scrap

Flower Center
Cut 1 yellow scrap

Flower Motif

PEPPERMINT CANDY CHRISTMAS

Log Cabin blocks with red-and-white stripe fabric for the last row give the look of candy canes to this star-shaped tree skirt.

DESIGN BY BARBARA CLAYTON

PROJECT SPECIFICATIONS

Skill Level: Intermediate
Tree Skirt Size: 48¼" x 48¼"
Block Size: 10" x 10"
Number of Blocks: 8

MATERIALS

- Fat eighth red mottled
- ⅛ yard white with red medium dots
- ⅛ yard white with red small dots
- ⅛ yard bright red tonal
- ¼ yard green mottled
- ¼ yard white with red print
- ¼ yard white with red outlines
- ½ yard red/white stripes
- ¾ yard red print
- ⅞ yard burgundy tonal
- Batting 50" x 50"
- Backing 50" x 50"
- Red all-purpose thread
- Red and green rayon thread
- Red and white quilting thread
- Clear nylon monofilament
- ½ yard fusible web
- ⅝ yard fabric stabilizer or paper
- Basic sewing tools and supplies

CUTTING

1. Prepare template for A using pattern given on page 139; cut as directed on the piece.

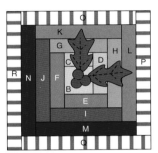

Candy-Stripe Log Cabin
10" x 10" Block
Make 8

2. Trace the leaf and berries shapes onto the paper side of the fusible web as directed on the patterns; cut out shapes, leaving a margin all around.

3. Fuse the shapes to the wrong sides of fabrics as directed on each piece; cut out on traced lines. Remove paper backing.

4. Cut eight 1½" by fabric width strips red/white stripes for O, P, Q and R.

5. Cut 1½" by fabric width strips for log pieces as follows: four burgundy tonal (M/N), three red print (I/J) and two bright red tonal (E/F).

6. Cut 1½" by fabric width strips for logs as follows: four white with red outlines (K/L) and three white with red print (G/H).

7. Cut two 1½" by fabric width strips white with red medium dots (C/D).

8. Cut one 2½" by fabric width strip white with red small dots; subcut strip into eight 2½" B squares.

9. Cut eight 6" x 6" squares fabric stabilizer or paper.

COMPLETING THE LOG CABIN BLOCKS

1. Place the B squares right sides together on a C/D strip and stitch as shown in Figure 1; trim edges even with B to complete eight units as shown in Figure 2. Press B to the right side with seam toward strip.

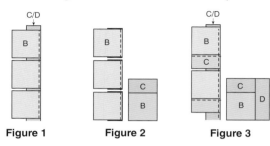

Figure 1   **Figure 2**   **Figure 3**

2. Repeat step 1 with the stitched unit and the remainder of the C/D strips as shown in Figure 3.

3. Continue sewing the stitched unit to strips in alphabetical order and trimming and pressing to complete a total of eight block backgrounds referring to Figure 4.

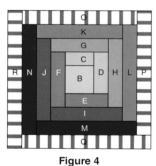

Figure 4

4. Arrange and fuse a holly/berries motif in the center of each block background referring to the pattern and block drawing for positioning of pieces.

5. Pin a 6" x 6" square fabric stabilizer or paper under the light pieces on the back side of each block background.

6. Using a close, wide zigzag stitch, machine-stitch around each leaf and along vein lines with green rayon thread, and around the berries and along the interior berry lines with red rayon thread.

7. When stitching is complete, remove fabric stabilizer or paper to complete the eight Candy-Stripe Log Cabin blocks.

COMPLETING THE TREE SKIRT

1. Join one each burgundy tonal and red print A pieces, stopping stitching at the end of the seam allowance as shown in Figure 5; repeat with remaining A pieces to make four A units.

Figure 5

2. Join two A units to make a half-star unit, stopping stitching at the end of the seam allowance as in step 1.

3. Join the two half-star units, stopping stitching at the end of the seam allowance, to complete the star center as shown in Figure 6; press seams in one direction.

Figure 6   **Figure 7**

4. With the K/L/O/P sides against the star points, pin and stitch a Candy-Stripe Log Cabin block between each star point, starting stitching at the inside points and working toward the outside as shown in Figure 7; press seams toward blocks.

5. Repeat step 4 with the remaining blocks to complete the pieced top.

6. Trace the circle cutout pattern onto paper and cut out; fold and crease the paper circle in half and then in half again. Repeat to divide the circle into eight equal parts.

7. Open and pin the creased paper flat on the pieced top, aligning creases with center seams as shown in Figure 8.

Figure 8

8. Mark a straight line from point to point through one A piece, again referring to Figure 8; cut along the marked line and around the pinned circle to cut the side and center openings.

9. Place the batting on a flat surface with the prepared backing square right side up on top; place the pieced top right sides together with the backing and pin to secure layers together.

10. Stitch all around outside edges, leaving a 6" opening on one side of the straight opening; trim points and clip into inside corners as shown in Figure 9.

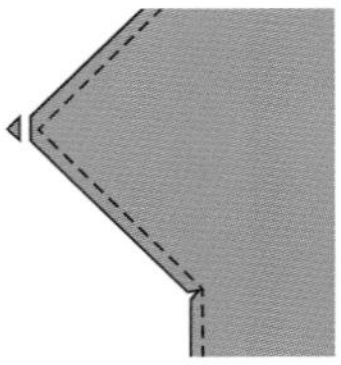

Figure 9

11. Turn right side out through the opening; press edges flat. Turn opening seam to the inside ¼" and hand-stitch opening closed,

12. Pin layers together to keep flat for quilting. Quilt as desired by hand or machine. **Note:** *The project shown was machine-quilted with clear nylon monofilament around the appliqué shapes and in the ditch of seams joining blocks and A pieces. It was quilted with white quilting thread in the ditch of seams of red pieces, in a 1" diagonal grid ¼" away from seams on A pieces and around outside edges of all striped pieces. It was quilted with red quilting thread in the ditch of seams of all light pieces and ¼" around the appliqué motifs.* ∎

Peppermint Candy Christmas
Placement Diagram 48¼" x 48¼"

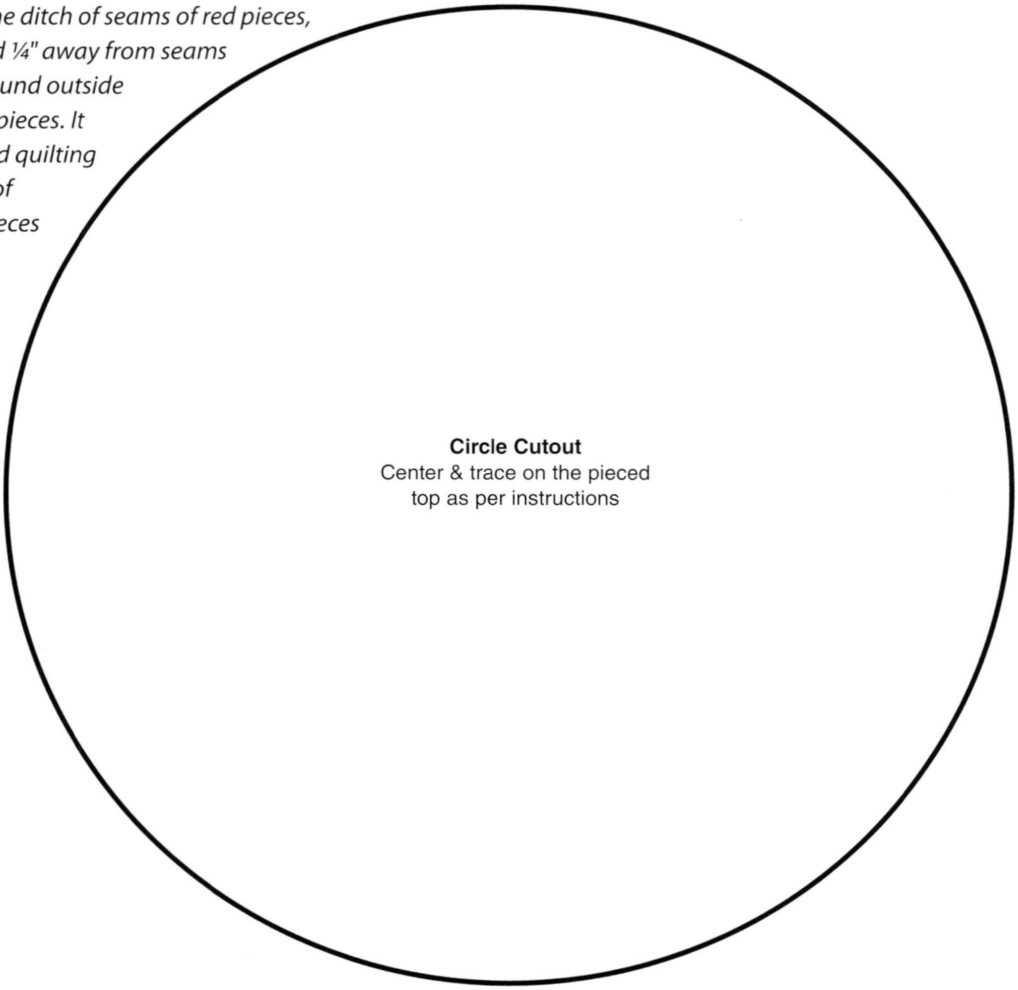

Circle Cutout
Center & trace on the pieced
top as per instructions

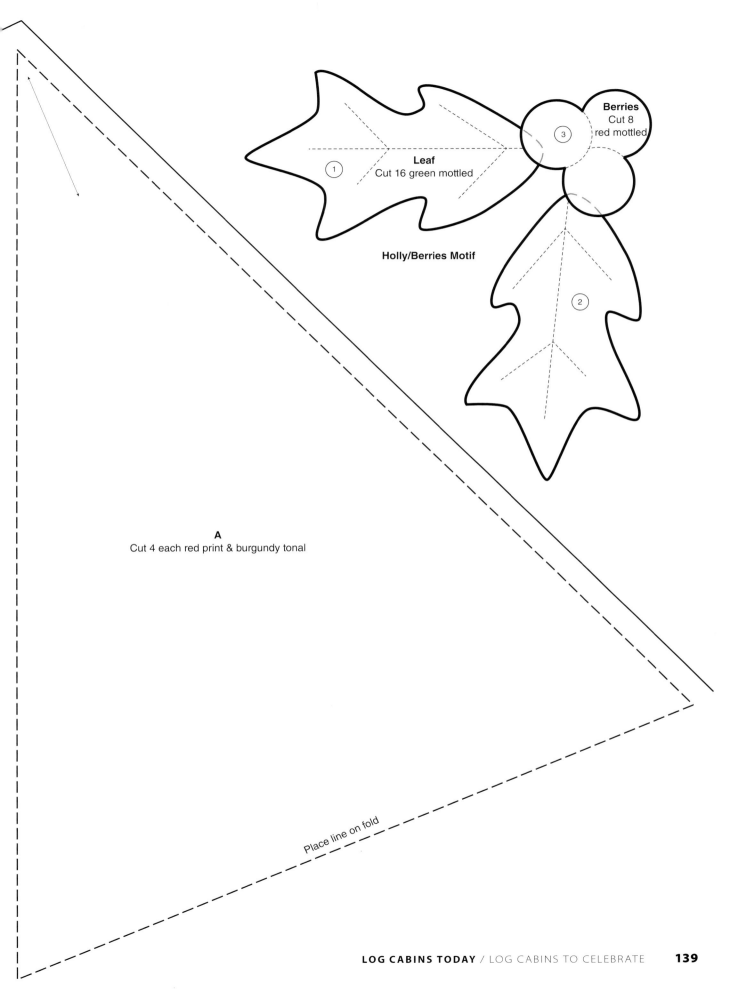

Berries
Cut 8
red mottled

Leaf
Cut 16 green mottled

Holly/Berries Motif

A
Cut 4 each red print & burgundy tonal

Place line on fold

CABINS OF DEMOCRACY

Remember the part quilting played in our country's history. Placement of the Star Cabin blocks gives this throw a layered, almost dimensional look.

DESIGN BY JULIE WEAVER

PROJECT NOTES

The 4" star units in the larger blocks were completed before placing on the fabric foundation square. Using the foundation to add the strips around the star unit helped to keep everything squared and subsequent sections of the block fit together well.

In spite of the fact that all of the cream and red strips were cut to the exact size needed, when finished, some of the blocks required more trimming than others to make them 8½" x 8½" square.

Before constructing the star units, choose the pieces that will be the outside corner Star blocks. The coordinating 1½" squares cut to go with these blocks will not be used. Sort the rest of the blue star pieces and red strips into 16 piles so you do not end up with two blocks of the same fabric.

PROJECT SPECIFICATIONS

Skill Level: Advanced Beginner
Quilt Size: 47" x 47"
Block Sizes: 4" x 4" and 8" x 8"
Number of Blocks: 4 and 16

MATERIALS

- 1 fat eighth or scraps 10 different blue prints
- 1 fat eighth or scraps 8 different red prints
- ⅝ yard navy floral
- 1 yard cream print
- 1⅛ yards blue print

Star
4" x 4" Block
Make 4

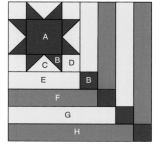

Star Cabin
8" x 8" Block
Make 16

- 1¼ yards light solid for foundation squares
- Batting 55" x 55"
- Backing 55" x 55"
- All-purpose thread to match fabrics
- Basic sewing tools and supplies

CUTTING

1. Cut three 1½" by fabric width strips cream print; subcut strips into (80) 1½" D squares

2. Cut three 2½" by fabric width strips cream print; subcut strips into (80) 1½" C rectangles.

3. Cut (10) 1½" by fabric width strips cream print; subcut strips into (32) 4½" E strips and (32) 6½" G strips.

4. From each of the 10 different blue prints, cut two 2½" x 2½" A squares and (24) 1½" x 1½" B squares. **Note:** Keep same blue print fabrics together.

5. From each of the eight different red prints, cut four 1½" x 5½" F strips and four 1½" x 7½" H strips. **Note:** Each red print is used in two blocks.

6. Cut a total of (25) 1½" x 1½" J squares from the eight different red prints.

7. Cut two 8½" by fabric width strips blue print; subcut strips into (40) 1½" I strips.

8. Cut five 1½" by fabric width strips blue print. Join strips on short ends to make a long strip; press seams open. Subcut strip into two 45½" L strips and two 47½" M strips.

9. Cut five 2¼" by fabric width strips blue print for binding.

10. Cut four 4½" x 37½" K strips navy floral.

11. Cut four 10" by fabric width strips light solid; subcut strips into (16) 10" foundation squares.

COMPLETING THE STAR BLOCKS/UNITS

1. To complete one Star block/unit, select eight same-fabric B squares. Draw a diagonal line from corner to corner on the wrong side of each square.

2. Place a B square right sides together on one end of a C rectangle and stitch on the marked line as shown in Figure 1; trim seam to ¼" and press B to the right side, again referring to Figure 1.

Figure 1

3. Repeat step 2 with a second B square on the opposite end of C to complete a B-C unit referring to Figure 2.

Figure 2

4. Repeat steps 2 and 3 to complete four B-C units.

5. Select an A square to match the B squares. Sew a B-C unit to opposite sides of A as shown in Figure 3; press seams toward A.

Figure 3   **Figure 4**

6. Sew a D square to opposite ends of a B-C unit to make a row as shown in Figure 4; press seams toward D. Repeat to make a second row.

7. Sew a B-C-D row to opposite sides of the A-B-C row to complete one Star block/unit as shown in Figure 5.

8. Repeat steps 1–7 to complete a total of 20 Star block/units. Set aside 4 Star blocks for corners.

Figure 5

COMPLETING THE STAR CABIN BLOCKS

1. To make one Star Cabin block, select one foundation square, one Star unit, four B squares to match the blue in the Star unit, two each E and G strips and two each matching F and H strips.

2. Pin the Star unit to the foundation square ¾" in from the top and left-side edge as shown in Figure 6.

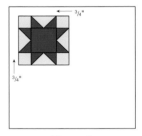

Figure 6

3. Sew a B square to one end of one E, F, G and H strip as shown in Figure 7; press seams toward B squares.

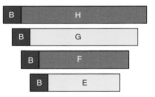

Figure 7

4. Place the E strip right sides together on the Star unit and stitch as shown in Figure 8; press E to the right side, again referring to Figure 8.

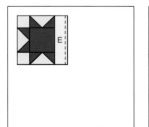

Figure 8

5. Sew the B-E strip to the bottom edge of the Star unit as shown in Figure 9; press B-E to the right side, again referring to Figure 9.

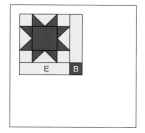

Figure 9

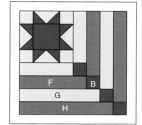

Figure 10

6. Continue adding the F, B-F, G, B-G, H and B-H strips to the foundation as in steps 4 and 5 and referring to Figure 10.

7. Trim block to 8½" x 8½" to complete.

8. Repeat steps 1–7 to complete a total of 16 Star Cabin blocks.

COMPLETING THE QUILT

1. Select four Star Cabin blocks and five I strips. Join as shown in Figure 11 to make an X row. Press seams toward I strips. Repeat to make a second X row.

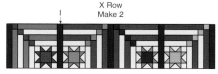

Figure 11

2. Select four Star Cabin blocks and five I strips. Join as shown in Figure 12 to make a Y row; press seams toward I strips. Repeat to make a second Y row.

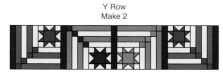

Figure 12

3. Join four I strips with five J squares to make a sashing row; press seams toward I strips. Repeat to make a total of five sashing rows.

4. Join the X and Y rows with the sashing rows referring to Figure 13 to complete the pieced center; press seams toward sashing rows.

Figure 13

5. Sew a K strip to opposite sides of the pieced center; press seams toward K strips.

6. Sew a Star block to each end of each remaining K strip; press seams toward K strips.

7. Sew a Star/K strip to the top and bottom of the pieced center; press seams toward strips.

8. Sew an L strip to the top and bottom and M strips to opposite sides of the pieced center to complete the pieced top; press seams toward L and M strips.

9. Layer, quilt and bind referring to Finishing Your Quilt on page 173. ■

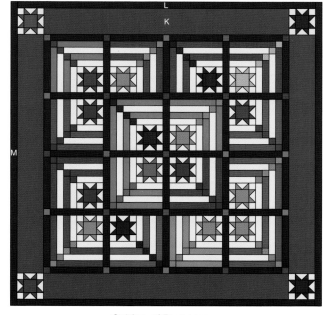

Cabins of Democracy
Placement Diagram 47" x 47"

APPLE OF MY EYE

Courthouse Steps is the best-known variation of the Log Cabin block. In this quilt, they are used as a pieced border. Alternating the orientation of the blocks adds the perfect finishing touch to the quilt.

DESIGN BY WENDY SHEPPARD

Courthouse Steps
4" x 4" Block
Make 28

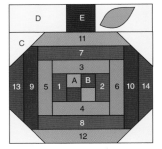

Apple
20" x 20" Block
Make 1

PROJECT SPECIFICATIONS

Skill Level: Intermediate
Quilt Size: 36" x 36"
Block Sizes: 20" x 20", 4" x 4"
Number of Blocks: 1 and 28

MATERIALS

- 4½" x 3½" scrap brown tonal (E)
- Fat eighth each pale yellow tonal and yellow solid
- Assorted red scraps
- ⅜ yard light green tonal
- ½ yard teal tonal
- ⅝ yard cream tonal
- ⅔ yard red print
- Batting 44" x 44"
- Backing 44" x 44"
- All-purpose thread to match fabrics
- Quilting thread
- Scrap fusible web
- Basic sewing tools and supplies

CUTTING

1. Cut three 1½" x 21" strips pale yellow tonal; subcut strips into (56) 1" strips for pieces 1 and 2 for the Courthouse Steps blocks.

2. Cut three 2½" x 21" strips yellow solid; subcut strips into (56) 1" strips for pieces 5 and 6 for the Courthouse Steps blocks.

3. Cut the following 2½"-wide strips from the assorted red scraps for the Apple block: two 2½" A squares, two 4½" for pieces 1 and 2, four 8½" for pieces 3, 4, 5 and 6,

four 12½" for pieces 7, 8, 9 and 10 and four 16½" for pieces 11, 12, 13 and 14.

4. Cut (28) 1½" x 1½" J squares from the assorted red scraps.

5. Cut a total of (56) 1" x 4½" strips from the assorted red scraps for pieces 11 and 12 for the Courthouse Steps blocks.

6. Cut three 1½" by fabric width strips light green tonal; subcut strips into two 20½" F strips and two 22½" G strips.

7. Cut two 2½" by fabric width strips light green tonal; subcut strips into (56) 1" strips for pieces 3 and 4 for Courthouse Steps blocks.

8. Cut four 1½" by fabric width strips teal tonal; subcut strips into two 22½" H strips and two 24½" I strips.

9. Cut two 3½" by fabric width strips teal tonal; subcut strips into (56) 1" strips for pieces 7 and 8 for Courthouse Steps blocks.

10. Trace the leaf shape onto the paper side of the scrap of fusible web; cut out, leaving a margin all around.

11. Fuse the shape to the wrong side of the teal tonal; cut out on traced lines. Remove paper backing.

12. Cut one 5" by fabric width strip cream tonal; subcut strip into four 5" C squares. Trim remainder of strip to 4½" and cut two 8½" D rectangles.

13. Cut two 3½" by fabric width strips cream tonal; subcut strips into (56) 1" strips for pieces 9 and 10 for Courthouse Steps blocks.

14. Cut four 2½" by fabric width strips red print; subcut strips into two 32½" K strips and two 36½ L strips.

15. Cut two 2½" B squares from the leftover from the strips cut in step 14.

16. Cut four 2¼" by fabric width strips red print for binding.

COMPLETING THE APPLE BLOCK

1. Select two each A and B squares, four C squares, two D rectangles, the E rectangle and all 2½"-wide assorted red pieces 1–14 that are designated in step 3 of Cutting for the Apple block.

2. Sew A to B; press seam toward B. Repeat to make a second unit. Join the two units to complete the center A-B unit as shown in Figure 1; press seam to one side.

Figure 1   **Figure 2**

3. Sew strips 1 and 2 to opposite sides of the A-B unit as shown in Figure 2; press seams toward strips. Repeat with strips 3 and 4 on the remaining sides of the A-B unit to complete one round as shown in Figure 2.

4. Continue to add strips around the A-B unit in numerical order to complete the apple unit referring to Figure 3 for order of piecing; press seams toward strips as added.

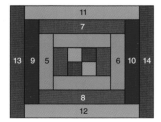

Figure 3

5. Draw a diagonal line from corner to corner on the wrong side of each C square.

6. Place a C square right sides together on each corner of the pieced apple unit and stitch on the marked lines as shown in Figure 4; trim seams to ¼" and press C to the right side, again referring to Figure 4.

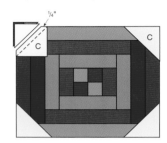

Figure 4

7. Sew E between two D rectangles; press seams toward D.

8. Sew the D-E strip to one long edge of the pieced apple unit referring to the block drawing; press seam toward the D-E strip.

9. Arrange the leaf shape on D and fuse in place referring to the block drawing for positioning; machine-stitch close to edges with a narrow satin stitch and thread to match fabric to complete the Apple block.

COMPLETING THE COURTHOUSE STEPS BLOCKS

1. To complete one Courthouse Steps block, select one J and the 1"-wide strips numbered 1–12 designated for the Courthouse Steps blocks.

2. Sew strips 1 and 2 to opposite sides of J; press seams toward strips. Repeat with strips 3 and 4 on the remaining sides of J to complete one round as shown in Figure 5.

Figure 5

3. Continue to add strips around the J square in numerical order to complete one Courthouse Steps block referring to Figure 6 for order of piecing; press seams toward strips as added.

Figure 6

4. Repeat steps 1–3 to complete a total of 28 Courthouse Steps blocks.

COMPLETING THE QUILT

1. Sew F strips to the top and bottom, and G strips to opposite sides, of the Apple block; press seams toward F and G strips.

2. Sew H strips to the top and bottom, and I strips to opposite sides, of the Apple block; press seams toward H and I strips.

3. Join six Courthouse Steps blocks as shown in Figure 7 to make a side strip; press seams in one direction. Repeat to make a second side strip.

Make 2

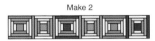

Figure 7

4. Sew the side strips to opposite sides of the bordered Apple block referring to the Placement Diagram for positioning of side strips; press seams toward I strips.

5. Join eight Courthouse Steps blocks as shown in Figure 8 to make the top strip; press seams in one direction. Repeat to make the bottom strip.

Make 2

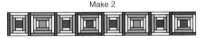

Figure 8

6. Sew the top strip to the top and the bottom strip to the bottom of the bordered Apple block to complete the pieced center referring to the Placement Diagram for positioning of strips; press seams toward H strips.

7. Sew K strips to opposite sides and L strips to the top and bottom of the pieced center to complete the quilt top; press seams toward K and L strips.

8. Layer, quilt and bind referring to Finishing Your Quilt on page 173. ◼

Apple of My Eye
Placement Diagram 36" x 36"

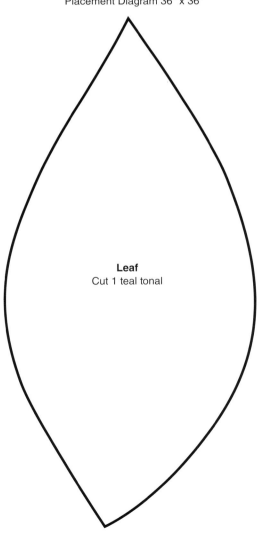

Leaf
Cut 1 teal tonal

PUMPKIN PATCH TABLE RUNNER

This pumpkin patch has three sizes of pumpkins. Using the Log Cabin block to create a picture or an object, like a pumpkin, shows the versatility of the block.

DESIGN BY WENDY SHEPPARD

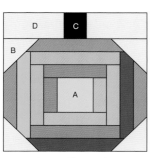

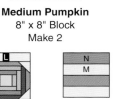

Medium Pumpkin
8" x 8" Block
Make 2

Large Pumpkin
16" x 16" Block
Make 1

Small Pumpkin
4" x 4" Block
Make 4

Rail Fence
4" x 4" Block
Make 8

PROJECT SPECIFICATIONS

Skill Level: Advanced Beginner
Runner Size: 44" x 22"
Block Sizes: 16" x 16", 8" x 8" and 4" x 4"
Number of Blocks: 1, 2 and 12

MATERIALS

- 1 fat quarter yellow print
- 1 fat eighth black solid
- ¼ yard black pin dot
- ⅝ yard cream solid
- Orange/yellow/gold fabrics to total 1½ yards
- Batting 52" x 30"
- Backing 52" x 30"
- All-purpose thread to match fabrics
- Quilting thread
- Basic sewing tools and supplies

CUTTING

1. Cut the following 2"-wide strips from the orange/yellow/gold fabrics for the Large Pumpkin block: two 4½" for pieces 1 and 2, and four 7½" for pieces 3, 4, 5 and 6, four 10½" for pieces 7, 8, 9 and 10 and four 13½" for pieces 11, 12, 13 and 14.

2. Cut the following 1¼"-wide strips from the orange/yellow/gold fabrics for the Medium Pumpkin blocks: four 2½" for pieces 1 and 2, eight 4" for pieces 3, 4, 5 and 6, eight 5½" for pieces 7, 8, 9 and 10 and eight 6½" for pieces 11, 12, 13 and 14.

3. Cut the following ⅞"-wide strips from the orange/yellow/gold fabrics for the Small Pumpkin blocks: eight 1½" for pieces 1 and 2, (16) 2¼" for pieces 3, 4, 5 and 6, (16) 3" for pieces 7, 8, 9 and 10 and (16) 3¾" for pieces 11, 12, 13 and 14.

4. Cut (16) 1½" x 4½" N strips from the orange/yellow/gold fabrics.

5. Cut two 2" x 18½" R strips orange/yellow/gold fabrics.

6. From the remaining orange/yellow/gold fabrics, cut and piece two 2½" x 44½" S strips.

7. From the remaining orange/yellow/gold fabrics, cut and piece 2¼"-wide binding strips to total 144".

8. Cut the following from black solid: one 3" x 3½" C, two 1¾" x 2" H and four 1¼" x 1" L.

9. Cut one 4½" by fabric width strip cream solid; subcut strip into four 4½" B squares and two 3½" x 7¼" D rectangles.

10. Cut two 2½" by fabric width strips cream solid; subcut strip into eight 2½" F squares, four 2" x 3⅞" G rectangles, (16) 1½" J squares and eight 1¼" x 2¼" K rectangles.

11. Cut two 1½" by fabric width strips cream solid; subcut strips into three 16½" O strips.

12. Cut one 4½" by fabric width strip cream solid; subcut strip into (16) 1½" M strips.

13. Cut three 1½" by fabric width strips black pin dot; subcut strips into two 39½" P strips and two 18½" Q strips.

14. From the yellow print, cut one 4½" x 4½" A square, two 2½" x 2½" E squares and four 1½" x 1½" I squares.

COMPLETING THE LARGE PUMPKIN BLOCK

1. Select one A square, four B squares, one C rectangle, two D rectangles and the 2"-wide strips numbered 1–14 cut in step 1 of Cutting.

2. Sew strips 1 and 2 to opposite sides of A; press seams toward strips. Repeat with strips 3 and 4 on the remaining sides of A to complete one round as shown in Figure 1.

Figure 1

3. Continue to add strips around the A square in numerical order to complete the pumpkin unit referring to Figure 2 for order of piecing; press seams toward strips as added.

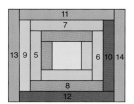

Figure 2

4. Draw a diagonal line from corner to corner on the wrong side of each B square.

5. Place a B square right sides together on each corner of the pieced pumpkin unit and stitch on the marked lines as shown in Figure 3; trim seams to ¼" and press B to the right side, again referring to Figure 3.

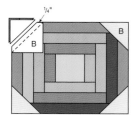

Figure 3

6. Sew C between two D rectangles; press seams toward C.

7. Sew the C-D strip to one long edge of the pieced pumpkin unit referring to the block drawing to complete the Large Pumpkin block.

COMPLETING THE MEDIUM PUMPKIN BLOCKS

1. To complete one Medium Pumpkin block, select one E square, four F squares, one H rectangle, two G rectangles and the 1¼"-wide strips numbered 1–14 cut in step 2 of Cutting.

2. Sew strips 1 and 2 to opposite sides of E; press seams toward strips. Repeat with strips 3 and 4 on the remaining sides of E to complete one round as shown in Figure 4.

Figure 4

3. Continue to add strips around the E square in numerical order to complete the pumpkin unit referring to Figure 5 for order of piecing; press seams toward strips as added.

Figure 5

4. Draw a diagonal line from corner to corner on the wrong side of each F square.

5. Place an F square right sides together on each corner of the pieced pumpkin unit and stitch on the marked lines as shown in Figure 6; trim seams to ¼" and press F to the right side, again referring to Figure 6.

Figure 6

6. Sew H between two G rectangles; press seams toward H.

7. Sew the G-H strip to one long edge of the pieced pumpkin unit referring to the block drawing to complete one Medium Pumpkin block.

8. Repeat steps 1–7 to complete a second Medium Pumpkin block.

COMPLETING THE SMALL PUMPKIN BLOCKS

1. To complete one Small Pumpkin block, select one I square, four J squares, one L rectangle, two K rectangles and the ⅞"-wide strips numbered 1–14 cut in step 3 of Cutting.

2. Sew strips 1 and 2 to opposite sides of I; press seams toward strips. Repeat with strips 3 and 4 on the remaining sides of I to complete one round as shown in Figure 7.

Figure 7

3. Continue to add strips around the I square in numerical order to complete the pumpkin unit referring to Figure 8 for order of piecing; press seams toward strips as added.

Figure 8

4. Draw a diagonal line from corner to corner on the wrong side of each J square.

5. Place a J square right sides together on each corner of the pieced pumpkin unit and stitch on the marked lines as shown in Figure 9; trim seams to ¼" and press J to the right side, again referring to Figure 9.

Figure 9

6. Sew L between two K rectangles; press seams toward K.

7. Sew the L-K strip to one long edge of the pieced pumpkin unit referring to the block drawing to complete one Small Pumpkin block.

8. Repeat steps 1–7 to complete a total of four Small Pumpkin blocks.

COMPLETING THE RAIL FENCE BLOCKS

1. Select two N and two M strips.

2. Alternate and join strips referring to the Rail Fence block drawing to complete one Rail Fence block; press seams toward N strips.

3. Repeat steps 1 and 2 to complete a total of eight Rail Fence blocks.

COMPLETING THE QUILT

1. Join four Rail Fence blocks to make a Rail Fence row as shown in Figure 10; press seams in one direction. Repeat to make a second row.

Make 2

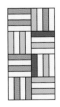

Figure 10   **Figure 11**

2. Join the two Rail Fence rows to complete the Rail Fence unit as shown in Figure 11; press seam to one side.

3. Join two Medium Pumpkin blocks to make a medium row as shown in Figure 12; press seam to one side.

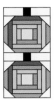

Figure 12   **Figure 13**

4. Join the four Small Pumpkin blocks to make a small row as shown in Figure 13; press seams in one direction.

5. Join the rows with the O strips and the Large Pumpkin block to complete the pieced center as shown in Figure 14; press seams toward O strips.

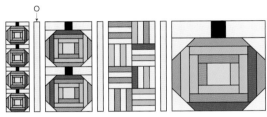

Figure 14

6. Sew P strips to the top and bottom, and Q strips to opposite short ends of the pieced center; press seams toward P and Q strips.

7. Sew R strips to opposite short ends and S strips to the top and bottom of the pieced center; press seams toward R and S strips.

8. Layer, quilt and bind referring to Finishing Your Quilt on page 173. ■

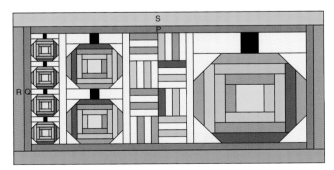

Pumpkin Patch Table Runner
Placement Diagram 44" x 22"

ON THE TOWN SQUARE

Use 2½" precut fabric strips to make this bed quilt quickly. An oversized Log Cabin block on point, framed with more strips, creates this unique medallion quilt.

DESIGN BY BEV GETSCHEL
QUILTED BY LYNETTE GELLING

PROJECT NOTES

Although this quilt appears to be scrappy and unplanned, the larger corner triangles do have the same fabric strips on the outer edges. If you want to duplicate that part of the quilt, careful planning and placement is necessary. We have included a drawing for each of these corner triangles showing the sizes and placement of the fabrics. We also recommend assigning letters to these fabrics, as we have in the instructions and drawings.

PROJECT SPECIFICATIONS

Skill Level: Intermediate
Quilt Size: 88" x 100"
Block Size: 12" x 12"
Number of Blocks: 5

MATERIALS

- 120 precut 2½"-wide coordinating fabrics with at least 13 matching pairs
- ⅞ yard black floral print
- 2⅛ yards black print
- Batting 96" x 108"
- Backing 96" x 108"
- Neutral-color all-purpose thread
- Quilting thread
- Basic sewing tools and supplies

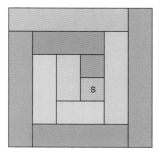

Small Log Cabin
12" x 12" Block
Make 5

CUTTING

1. Select and set aside 10 dark precut 2½"-wide strips for binding.

2. Select three 2½" precut strips; assign a letter label to each strip starting with the letter A and ending with the letter C.

3. Cut the following from the strips labeled in step 2: one each 19½" and 21½" A and C and two 19½" B.

4. Sort the precut 2½"-wide strips into 13 matching pairs for framing the R triangles. Give a letter label to each strip pair starting with the letter A and ending with the letter P.

5. Cut two of each of the following sizes from the strip pairs labeled in step 4: 21½" D, 23½" F, 25½" H, 27½" J, 29½" L, 31½" N and 33½" P. ***Note:*** *You need two matching strips for each letter to create the R corner triangles to match on sides later.*

6. Cut one of each of the following sizes from the strip pairs labeled in step 4: 23½" and 25½" E, 23½" and 25½" G, 27½" and 29½" I, 27½" and 29½" K, 31½" and 33½" M and 31½" and 33½" O.

7. Cut one 8½" strip for strip 1 and one 40½" strip for the last strip, and two each of the following size strips from 2½"-wide precut strips as follows for framing the center Q square: 10½", 12½", 14½", 16½", etc., adding 2" to each size, ending with size 38½".

8. Cut (10) 2½" S squares from 2½"-wide precut strips.

9. Cut 10 each of the following sizes from the 2½"-wide precut strips for the pieces for the Small Log Cabin blocks: 4½", 6½", 8½" and 10½".

10. Cut five 12½" strips from the 2½"-wide precut strips for the last pieces for the Small Log Cabin blocks.

11. Cut the remaining 2½"-wide precut strips into (172) 8½" U strips.

12. Cut one 17½" by fabric width strip black floral; subcut strip into two 17½" squares. Cut each square in half on one diagonal to make four R triangles.

13. Cut one 8½" by fabric width strip black floral; subcut strip into one 8½" Q square.

14. Cut four 6½" x 72½" T strips along the length of the black print.

COMPLETING THE LOG CABIN CENTER UNIT

1. Using strips cut in step 7 of Cutting, sew the 2½" x 8½" strip 1 to Q as shown in Figure 1; press seam away from Q.

Figure 1

2. Continue to add strips around Q, starting with the shortest strips, until you have eight strips on each side of Q to complete the Log Cabin center unit referring to Figures 2 and 3; press seams toward strips as added.

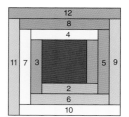

Figure 2

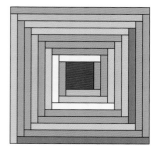

Figure 3

COMPLETING THE CORNER TRIANGLES

1. Using strips cut in steps 2–6 of Cutting, select one R triangle and lettered strips referring to Figure 4 for one of the R corner triangles.

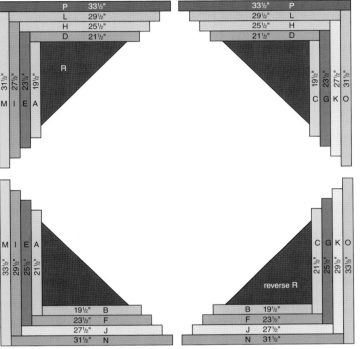

Figure 4

2. Align one end of the 19½" strip with the left edge of the square corner of R and stitch as shown in Figure 5. *Note: The strip will extend beyond the end of R; this will be trimmed later.* Press seam toward the strip.

Figure 5

3. Add a 21½" strip to the adjacent square side of R referring to Figure 6; press seam toward the strip.

Figure 6

4. Continue to add strips to R in the same manner referring to Figure 4 for placement and sizes; press seams toward strips as added.

5. Trim excess ends of strips even with the long edge of R as shown in Figure 7 to complete one R corner triangle.

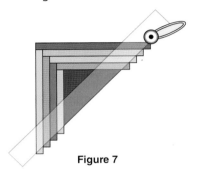

Figure 7

6. Repeat steps 1–5, again referring to Figure 4 for strips used in each triangle, to make a second R corner triangle and two reverse R corner triangles, starting the first strips on these on the right edge of R as shown in Figure 8.

Figure 8

COMPLETING THE SMALL LOG CABIN BLOCKS

1. Join two S squares; press seam to one side.

2. Using strips cut in step 9 of Cutting, add a 4½" strip to the S unit as shown in Figure 9; press seam toward the strip.

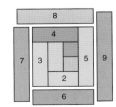

Figure 9   **Figure 10**

3. Continue to add strips around the S unit to complete one Small Log Cabin block as shown in Figure 10; press seams toward strips as added.

4. Repeat steps 1–3 to complete a total of five Small Log Cabin blocks.

COMPLETING THE QUILT

1. Center and sew an R corner triangle and a reverse R corner triangle to opposite sides of the Log Cabin center unit as shown in Figure 11; trim excess on each end even with the center unit as shown in Figure 12. Press seams toward the R corner triangle and the reverse R corner triangle.

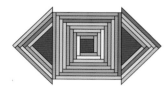

Figure 11

2. Repeat step 1, referring to Figure 12, to complete the pieced center.

Figure 12

3. Measure the pieced center and trim to 60½" x 60½" square, if necessary.

4. Join the five Small Log Cabin blocks to make a Log Cabin strip as shown in Figure 13; press seams in one direction.

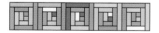

Figure 13

5. Sew the Log Cabin strip to the top edge of the pieced center as shown in Figure 14; press seam toward the pieced center.

Figure 14

6. Sew a T strip to opposite long sides and to the top and bottom of the pieced center; press seams toward T strips.

7. Join 42 U strips to make a side strip; press seams in one direction. Repeat to make a second side strip.

8. Sew side strips to opposite sides of the pieced center; press seams toward U strips.

9. Repeat step 7 with 44 U strips and sew the strips to the top and bottom of the pieced center to complete the pieced top.

10. Layer, quilt and bind referring to Finishing Your Quilt on page 173. ■

On the Town Square
Placement Diagram 88" x 100"

DOUBLE LIGHTNING

Using a red triangle as the starting point for each block, and only adding strips on two sides, creates a very different-looking Log Cabin block.

DESIGN BY GINA GEMPESAW
QUILTED BY CAROLE WHALING

PROJECT SPECIFICATIONS

Skill Level: Intermediate
Quilt Size: 74" x 86"
Block Size: 12" x 6"
Number of Blocks: 55

MATERIALS

- ¾ yard red brick print
- 1⅛ yards tan tonal
- 2⅛ yards brown spaced print
- 2¼ yards brown dot/print
- 2⅜ yards cream tonal
- Batting 82" x 94"
- Backing 82" x 94"
- All-purpose thread to match fabrics
- Basic sewing tools and supplies

CUTTING

1. Cut two 5¼" by width of fabric strips red brick print; subcut strips into (14) 5¼" squares. Cut each square on both diagonals to make 56 A triangles.

2. Cut seven 1½" by fabric width strips red brick print. Join strips on short ends to make one long strip; press seams open. Subcut strip into two 72½" H strips and two 62½" I strips.

3. Cut three 5⅛" by fabric width strips tan tonal; subcut strips into (55) 1⅞" strips. With the each rectangle right side up, cut the left end on the diagonal at a 45-degree angle to make angled B strips as shown in Figure 1.

Figure 1

Lightning
12" x 6" Block
Make 55

4. Cut three 6½" by fabric width strips tan tonal; subcut strips into (55) 1⅞" strips. With each rectangle right side up, cut the right end on the diagonal at a 45-degree angle to make angled C strips as shown in Figure 2.

Figure 2

5. Cut three 8" by fabric width strips brown spaced print; subcut strips into (55) 1⅞" D strips. With each rectangle right side up, cut the left end on the diagonal at a 45-degree angle to make angled D strips as shown in Figure 3.

Figure 3

6. Cut three 9⅜" by fabric width strips brown spaced print; subcut strips into (55) 1⅞" E strips. With each rectangle right side up, cut the right end on the diagonal at a 45-degree angle to make angled E strips as shown in Figure 4.

Figure 4

7. Cut eight 2¼" by fabric width strips brown spaced print for binding.

8. Cut four 6½" x 74½" J strips along the length of the brown dot/print.

9. Cut (10) 6⅞" by fabric width strips cream tonal; subcut strips into (55) 6⅞" squares. Cut each square in half on one diagonal to make 110 F triangles.

10. Cut two 6½" by fabric width strips cream tonal; subcut strips into (10) 6½" G squares.

COMPLETING THE BLOCKS

1. To complete one Lightning block, sew B to A as shown in Figure 5; press seam toward B.

Figure 5   **Figure 6**

2. Add C to the A-B unit as shown in Figure 6; press seam toward C.

3. Add D to the B side and E to the C side of the pieced unit referring to Figure 7; press seams toward D and then E.

Figure 7

4. Add F to the D and E sides of the pieced unit to complete one Lightning block referring to the block drawing; press seams toward F.

5. Repeat steps 1–4 to complete a total of 55 Lightning blocks.

COMPLETING THE QUILT

1. Select and join six Lightning blocks to make an X row as shown in Figure 8; press seams in one direction. Repeat to make a total of five X rows.

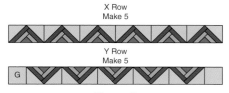

Figure 8

2. Select and join five Lightning blocks and add a G square to each end to make a Y row, again referring to Figure 8; press seams in one direction. Repeat to make a total of five Y rows.

3. Join one each X and Y row to make a row unit referring to Figure 9; repeat to make a total of five row units.

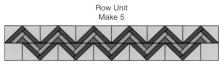

Figure 9

4. Join the row units to complete the pieced center referring to the Placement Diagram for positioning; press seams in one direction.

5. Sew H strips to opposite long sides and I strips to the top and bottom of the pieced center; press seams toward H and I strips.

6. Sew J strips to opposite long sides and to the top and bottom of the pieced center to complete the pieced top; press seams toward J strips.

7. Layer, quilt and bind referring to Finishing Your Quilt on page 173. ■

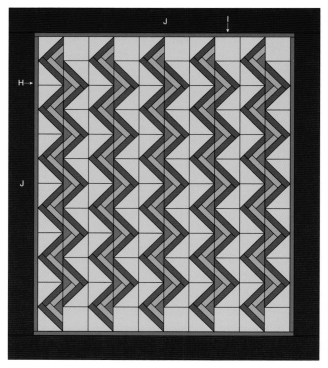

Double Lightning
Placement Diagram 74" x 86"

WINDFALL

Celebrate autumn with Crazy Log Cabin blocks made of strips of random sizes and shapes. The autumn leaves just fall across the surface.

DESIGN BY ARLENE BAUMAN

PROJECT SPECIFICATIONS

Skill Level: Intermediate
Quilt Size: 46½" x 63½"
Block Size: 12" x 12"
Number of Blocks: 6

MATERIALS

- Assorted varying width scrap strips for Crazy Log Cabin blocks and borders
- Assorted tonal scraps for appliquéd leaves
- ½ yard 4 different tonals to coordinate with scraps
- ⅞ yard coordinating print
- Batting 55" x 72"
- Backing 55" x 72"
- Neutral-color all-purpose thread
- Quilting thread
- Variegated thread to complement leaf appliqué
- Fusible web based on number of desired leaves
- 12½" x 12½" square ruler
- Basic sewing tools and supplies

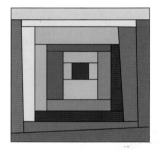

Crazy Log Cabin
12" x 12" Block
Make 6

CUTTING

1. Cut one 12½" by fabric width strip coordinating print; subcut strip into two 12½" A squares and two 6½" x 6½" D squares. Cut each D square in half on one diagonal to make four D triangles.

2. Cut one 12⅝" by fabric width strip coordinating print; subcut strip into two 12⅝" squares. Cut each square on both diagonals to make a total of eight B triangles. Set aside two of these triangles for another project.

Tips for Selecting Scraps

Most quilters have favorite colors and their scraps will reflect that. When selecting scraps for this project, you may coordinate the fabric colors for a theme, such as patriotic with reds, whites and blues, Christmas with reds and greens, or many other color combinations. The goal is to make a coordinated quilt using scraps.

The blocks may start with a square, a rectangle or even a pieced unit such as two joined

triangles that create a square. Making this type of quilt is the perfect way to use up lots of scraps.

To create the logs around the center shape, select coordinating or contrasting strips of different widths. These strips may be wider at one end than the other. The width should vary from at least ½" finished to not more than 2½" or 3".

3. Cut four 1½" by fabric width strips from each of the four tonals for C pieces.

4. Cut two 2¼" by fabric width strips from each of the four tonals for binding.

COMPLETING THE BLOCKS

1. Sort the scrap strips by length—shorter strips will be used closer to the block center while longer strips will be used on the outer edges. The longest strip must be at least 12½" long.

2. To complete one Crazy Log Cabin block, select a block center for piece 1 referring to Tips for Selecting Scraps.

3. Select one shorter scrap strip for piece 2; place piece 1 on piece 2 right sides together. Stitch piece 1 to piece 2 as shown in Figure 1. Flip piece 1 to the right side; finger-press seam toward piece 1.

Figure 1

4. Repeat step 3 with piece 3 on the opposite side of piece 1 as shown in Figure 2.

Figure 2

5. Continue to add strips to the opposite sides of the pieced unit until the block is at least 12½" on all sides; trim the pieced block to 12½" x 12½" square using the square ruler to complete one Crazy Log Cabin block as shown in Figure 3.

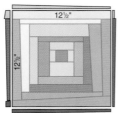

Figure 3

6. Repeat steps 2–5 to complete a total of six Crazy Log Cabin blocks.

COMPLETING THE SIDE & CORNER UNITS

1. Select one 1½"-wide tonal C strip; place a B triangle with the right-edge short side right sides together on the strip and stitch as shown in Figure 4.

Figure 4

2. Press the C strip to the right side with seam toward the strip; trim the C strip even with B on both ends as shown in Figure 5.

Figure 5

3. Repeat steps 1 and 2 with a second same-color C strip on the remaining short side of B as shown in Figure 6.

Figure 6

4. Repeat steps 1 and 2 with two different-color C strips to complete one B-C side unit as shown in Figure 7.

Figure 7

5. Repeat steps 1–4 to complete a total of six B-C side units.

6. Select one 1½"-wide C strip and one D triangle. Place the D triangle with the long edge right sides together with the C strip and stitch as shown in Figure 8.

Figure 8

7. Press the C strip to the right side with seam toward strip; trim the C strip even with D on both ends as shown in Figure 9.

Figure 9

8. Repeat steps 6 and 7 with a second different-color C strip to complete one C-D corner unit as shown in Figure 10.

Figure 10

9. Repeat steps 6–8 to complete a total of four C-D corner units.

COMPLETING THE QUILT

1. Arrange and join two Crazy Log Cabin blocks with one A square and one each B-C side and C-D corner units to make a row as shown in Figure 11; press seams away from the blocks. Repeat to make a second row.

Make 2

Figure 11

2. Sew a B-C side unit to opposite sides and a C-D corner unit to one remaining side of a Crazy Log Cabin block to make a block corner unit as shown in Figure 12; press seams away from the block. Repeat to make a second block corner unit.

Make 2

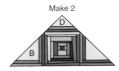

Figure 12

3. Arrange and join the two block rows with the corner block units as shown in Figure 13 to complete the quilt center; press seams in one direction.

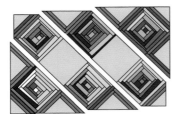

Figure 13

4. Cut the remaining 1½"-wide tonal strips into random lengths; select and join these lengths on the short ends to make one long strip. Press seams to one side.

5. Repeat step 4 with the 2¼"-wide binding strips. Measure out 235", cut and set aside for binding. Set aside remainder of the pieced strip for borders.

6. Subcut the 1½"-wide pieced strip into two strips each in the following sizes: 51½" E, 36½" F, 53½" G and 38½" H.

7. Sew the E strips to opposite long sides and F strips to the top and bottom of the quilt center; press seams toward E and F strips.

8. Sew the G strips to opposite long sides and H strips to the top and bottom of the quilt center; press seams toward G and H strips.

9. Gather all 1½"-wide and 2¼"-wide leftover strips and any other leftover pieces from making the blocks. Piece shorter strips together to make longer strips, pressing seams in one direction. Join the strips to make several large strip sets as shown in Figure 14.

4¾"

Figure 14

10. Subcut the strip sets into 4¾" segments, again referring to Figure 14.

12. Join the 4¾" segments on the 4¾" ends, varying the fabric placement and width of strips in the units to make two 59¾" I strips and two 42¾" J strips; press seams in one direction.

13. With beginning end of J strip even with quilt top, pin and stitch a J strip to the top of the quilt center, stopping stitching 2" from the end, leaving excess strip free as shown in Figure 15; press seam away from the J strip.

2"

J

Figure 15

14. Pin and stitch an I strip to the long side on the beginning end of the J strip and stitch as shown in Figure 16; press seam away from the I strip.

Figure 16

Windfall
Placement Diagram 46½" x 63½"

15. Repeat step 14 with a J strip on the bottom edge and an I strip on the remaining long side of the quilt center; press seams away from the I and J strips.

16. Pin the remainder of the top J strip over the stitched I strip and complete the seam to complete the pieced top referring to Figure 17.

Figure 17

17. Prepare templates for leaf shapes using patterns given. Trace shapes onto the paper side of the fusible web, tracing as many of each shape as desired. ***Note:*** *You may prefer not to have as many leaves on the center of your quilt as the sample, or you may want to spread your leaves over the entire top.*

18. Cut out traced shapes, leaving a margin around each one. Fuse shapes to the wrong side of the assorted scraps as desired. Cut out shapes on traced lines; remove paper backing.

19. Arrange the leaf shapes on the pieced top as desired; fuse in place.

20. Using variegated thread, machine-stitch pieces in place with a narrow, close blanket stitch.

21. Layer, quilt and bind referring to Finishing Your Quilt on page 173. ◼

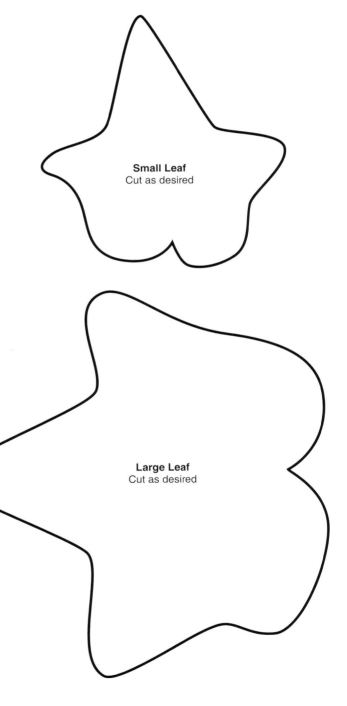

Small Leaf
Cut as desired

Large Leaf
Cut as desired

Medium Leaf
Cut as desired

MOD QUADS

The Courthouse Steps block is a traditional variation of the Log Cabin block. Using all blue fabric and blocks in two different shapes, gives it a totally new look in this modern throw.

DESIGNED & PIECED BY GINA GEMPESAW
MACHINE-QUILTED BY CAROLE WHALING

PROJECT SPECIFICATIONS

Skill Level: Intermediate
Quilt Size: 46" x 46"
Block Sizes: 9" x 9" and 9" x 18"
Number of Blocks: 8 and 4

MATERIALS

- ⅔ yard light blue tonal (A)
- 1⅛ yards dark blue print (B)
- 1¼ yards medium blue tonal stripe (C)
- Batting 54" x 54"
- Backing 54" x 54"
- Neutral-color all-purpose thread
- Basic sewing tools and supplies

CUTTING

1. Cut six 2" by fabric width strips light blue tonal (A); subcut strips into four 18½" A1 strips, eight 9½" A2 strips and eight 6½" A3 strips.

2. Cut two 3½" by fabric width strips light blue tonal (A); subcut strips into six 6½" A4 strips and four 3½" A5 squares.

3. Cut six 2" by fabric width strips dark blue print (B); subcut strips into four 18½" B1 strips, eight 9½" B2 strips and eight 6½" B3 strips.

4. Cut two 3½" by fabric width strips dark blue print (B); subcut strips into six 6½" B4 strips and four 3½" B5 squares.

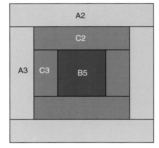

**Light Square
Courthouse Steps**
9" x 9" Block
Make 4

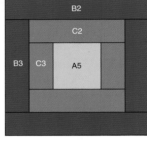

**Dark Square
Courthouse Steps**
9" x 9" Block
Make 4

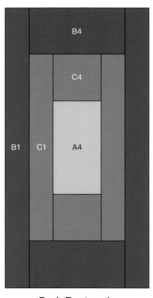

**Dark Rectangle
Courthouse Steps**
9" x 18" Block
Make 2

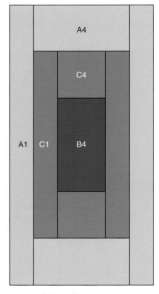

**Light Rectangle
Courthouse Steps**
9" x 18" Block
Make 2

5. Cut four 1½" by fabric width strips dark blue print (B); subcut strips into two 36½" B6 strips and two 38½" B7 strips.

6. Cut five 2¼" by fabric width strips dark blue print for binding.

7. Cut six 2" by fabric width strips medium blue tonal stripe (C); subcut strips into eight 12½" C1 strips, (16) 6½" C2 strips and (16) 3½" C3 strips.

8. Cut one 3½" by fabric width strips medium blue tonal stripe (C); subcut strip into eight 3½" C4 squares.

9. Cut five 4½" by fabric width strips medium blue tonal stripe (C). Trim two strips to 38½" for C5. Sew the remaining three strips together on short ends to make a long strip; press seams open. Subcut strip into two 46½" C6 strips.

COMPLETING THE SQUARE COURTHOUSE STEPS BLOCKS

1. To make one Dark Square Courthouse Steps block, select one A5 square and two each B2, B3, C2 and C3 strips.

2. Sew a C3 strip to opposite sides of A5 as shown in Figure 1; press seams toward C3 strips.

Figure 1

Figure 2

3. Sew a C2 strip to the remaining sides of A5 as shown in Figure 2; press seams toward C2 strips.

4. Sew B3 strips to the C3 sides and B2 strips to the C2 sides of the pieced unit to complete one Dark Square Courthouse Steps block referring to Figure 3; press seams toward the B3 and B2 strips.

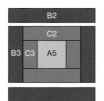

Figure 3

5. Repeat steps 1–4 to complete a total of four Dark Square Courthouse Steps blocks.

6. To make one Light Square Courthouse Steps, select one B5 square and two each A2, A3, C2 and C3 strips.

7. Sew the strips to the B5 square referring to Figure 4, pressing seams toward strips as added to complete one Light Square Courthouse Steps block.

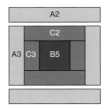

Figure 4

8. Repeat steps 6 and 7 to complete a total of four Light Square Courthouse Steps blocks.

COMPLETING THE RECTANGLE COURTHOUSE STEPS BLOCKS

1. To make one Light Rectangle Courthouse Steps block, select one B4 rectangle, two C4 squares and two each A1, A4 and C1 strips.

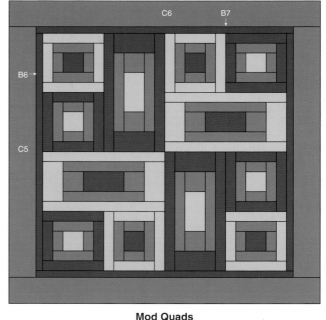

Mod Quads
Placement Diagram 46" x 46"

2. Sew a C4 square to each short end of B4 as shown in Figure 5; press seams toward C4.

3. Sew a C1 strip to opposite long sides of the pieced unit, again referring to Figure 5; press seams toward C1 strips.

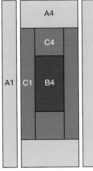

Figure 5   **Figure 6**

4. Sew A4 pieces to opposite short ends and A1 strips to opposite long sides of the pieced unit to complete one Light Rectangle Courthouse Steps block referring to Figure 6; press seams toward A4 and A1 strips.

5. Repeat steps 1–4 to complete a second Light Rectangle Courthouse Steps block.

6. To make one Dark Rectangle Courthouse Steps block, select one A4 rectangle, two C4 squares and two each B1, B4 and C1 strips.

7. Sew C4 squares to opposite short ends and C1 strips to opposite long sides of A4 referring to Figure 7; press seams toward C4 and C1.

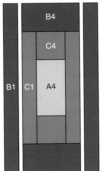

Figure 7   **Figure 8**

8. Sew B4 pieces to opposite short ends and B1 strips to opposite long sides of the pieced unit to complete one Dark Rectangle Courthouse Steps block referring to Figure 8; press seams toward B4 and B1 strips.

9. Repeat steps 6–8 to complete a second Dark Rectangle Courthouse Steps block.

COMPLETING THE QUILT

1. Join one each Light and Dark Square Courthouse Steps block with one Dark Rectangle Courthouse Steps block to make a dark block unit as shown in Figure 9; press seams toward dark blocks. Repeat to complete a second dark block unit.

Figure 9   **Figure 10**

2. Join one each Light and Dark Square Courthouse Steps blocks with a Light Rectangle Courthouse Steps block to make a light block unit as shown in Figure 10; press seams toward the dark block and then the Light Rectangle Courthouse Steps block. Repeat to complete a second light block unit.

3. Sew a dark block unit to a light block unit to make a row as shown in Figure 11; press seam toward the dark block unit. Repeat to complete a second row.

Make 2

Figure 11   **Figure 12**

4. Join the two rows referring to Figure 12 to complete the pieced center; press seam in one direction.

5. Sew a B6 strip to opposite sides and B7 strips to the top and bottom of the pieced center; press seams toward B6 and B7 strips.

6. Sew a C5 strip to opposite sides and C6 strips to the top and bottom of the pieced center to complete the pieced top; press seams toward strips.

7. Layer, quilt and bind referring to Finishing Your Quilt on page 173. ■

GO GREEN TABLE TOPPER

This design features a traditional Courthouse Steps block. Using strip sets instead of adding the logs individually makes this Log Cabin design extra easy and extra quick to complete.

DESIGN BY CONNIE RAND

PROJECT SPECIFICATIONS

Skill Level: Beginner
Topper Size: 32" x 32"
Block Size: 11" x 11"
Number of Blocks: 4

MATERIALS

- 1 fat quarter each light, medium and dark green prints or mottleds
- Scrap white-with-green print
- 1 yard black leaf print
- Batting 40" x 40"
- Backing 40" x 40"
- Neutral-color all-purpose thread
- Quilting thread
- Basic sewing tools and supplies

CUTTING

1. Cut four 2½" x 2½" A squares white-with-green print.

2. Cut each fat quarter into (17) 1" x 21" strips.

3. Cut two 5½" x 22½" F strips and two 5½" x 32½" G strips black leaf print.

4. Cut four 2½" by fabric width strips black leaf print for binding.

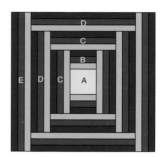

Go Green Courthouse Steps
11" x 11" Block
Make 4

COMPLETING THE BLOCKS

1. Join one each light, medium and dark green strips to make 17 strip sets; press seams toward darker strips.

2. Subcut strip sets into eight each 2½" B and 11½" E units and 16 each 5½" C and 8½" D units.

3. To complete one Go Green Courthouse Steps block, sew a B unit to opposite sides of A as shown in Figure 1; press seams toward A. Add C units to remaining sides of A as shown in Figure 2; press seams toward the C units.

Figure 1

Figure 2

4. Continue adding units referring to the block drawing, pressing seams toward strips as added, to complete one block.

5. Repeat steps 3 and 4 to complete a total of four Go Green Courthouse Steps blocks.

COMPLETING THE TABLE TOPPER

1. Join two blocks to make a row as shown in Figure 3; press seam to one side. Repeat to make a second row.

Figure 3

2. Join the rows to complete the pieced center referring to the Placement Diagram; press seam in one direction.

3. Sew F strips to opposite sides and G strips to top and bottom of the pieced center to complete the table topper; press seams toward F and G strips.

4. Layer, quilt and bind referring to Finishing Your Quilt on page 173. ■

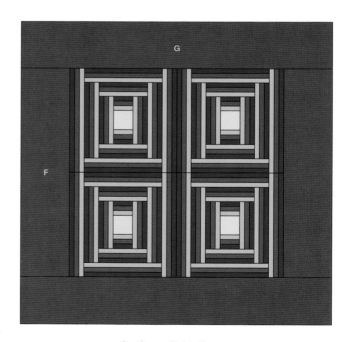

Go Green Table Topper
Placement Diagram 32" x 32"

FINISHING INSTRUCTIONS

When you have completed the quilt top as instructed, finish your quilt with these four easy steps.

1. Sandwich the batting between the completed top and prepared backing; pin or baste layers together to hold. ***Note:*** *If using basting spray to hold layers together, refer to instructions on the product container for use.*

2. Quilt as desired by hand or machine; remove pins or basting. Trim excess backing and batting even with quilt top.

3. Join binding strips on short ends to make one long strip. Fold the strip in half along length with wrong sides together; press.

4. Sew binding to quilt edges, mitering corners and overlapping ends. Fold binding to the back side and stitch in place to finish. ■

METRIC CONVERSION CHARTS

METRIC CONVERSIONS

Canada/U.S. Measurement		Multiplied by		Metric Measurement
yards	x	.9144	=	metres (m)
yards	x	91.44	=	centimetres (cm)
inches	x	2.54	=	centimetres (cm)
inches	x	25.40	=	millimetres (mm)
inches	x	.0254	=	metres (m)

Canada/U.S. Measurement		Multiplied by		Metric Measurement
centimetres	x	.3937	=	inches
metres	x	1.0936	=	yards

STANDARD EQUIVALENTS

Canada/U.S. Measurement		Metric Measurement		
⅛ inch	=	3.20 mm	=	0.32 cm
¼ inch	=	6.35 mm	=	0.635 cm
⅜ inch	=	9.50 mm	=	0.95 cm
½ inch	=	12.70 mm	=	1.27 cm
⅝ inch	=	15.90 mm	=	1.59 cm
¾ inch	=	19.10 mm	=	1.91 cm
⅞ inch	=	22.20 mm	=	2.22 cm
1 inch	=	25.40 mm	=	2.54 cm
⅛ yard	=	11.43 cm	=	0.11 m
¼ yard	=	22.86 cm	=	0.23 m
⅜ yard	=	34.29 cm	=	0.34 m
½ yard	=	45.72 cm	=	0.46 m
⅝ yard	=	57.15 cm	=	0.57 m
¾ yard	=	68.58 cm	=	0.69 m
⅞ yard	=	80.00 cm	=	0.80 m
1 yard	=	91.44 cm	=	0.91 m
1⅛ yards	=	102.87 cm	=	1.03 m
1¼ yards	=	114.30 cm	=	1.14 m

Canada/U.S. Measurement		Metric Measurement		
1⅜ yards	=	125.73 cm	=	1.26 m
1½ yards	=	137.16 cm	=	1.37 m
1⅝ yards	=	148.59 cm	=	1.49 m
1¾ yards	=	160.02 cm	=	1.60 m
1⅞ yards	=	171.44 cm	=	1.71 m
2 yards	=	182.88 cm	=	1.83 m
2⅛ yards	=	194.31 cm	=	1.94 m
2¼ yards	=	205.74 cm	=	2.06 m
2⅜ yards	=	217.17 cm	=	2.17 m
2½ yards	=	228.60 cm	=	2.29 m
2⅝ yards	=	240.03 cm	=	2.40 m
2¾ yards	=	251.46 cm	=	2.51 m
2⅞ yards	=	262.88 cm	=	2.63 m
3 yards	=	274.32 cm	=	2.74 m
3⅛ yards	=	285.75 cm	=	2.86 m
3¼ yards	=	297.18 cm	=	2.97 m
3⅜ yards	=	308.61 cm	=	3.09 m
3½ yards	=	320.04 cm	=	3.20 m
3⅝ yards	=	331.47 cm	=	3.31 m
3¾ yards	=	342.90 cm	=	3.43 m
3⅞ yards	=	354.32 cm	=	3.54 m
4 yards	=	365.76 cm	=	3.66 m
4⅛ yards	=	377.19 cm	=	3.77 m
4¼ yards	=	388.62 cm	=	3.89 m
4⅜ yards	=	400.05 cm	=	4.00 m
4½ yards	=	411.48 cm	=	4.11 m
4⅝ yards	=	422.91 cm	=	4.23 m
4¾ yards	=	434.34 cm	=	4.34 m
4⅞ yards	=	445.76 cm	=	4.46 m
5 yards	=	457.20 cm	=	4.57 m

PHOTO INDEX

9 Crack in the Wall

18 Radiant Star

27 La Luz Del Sol

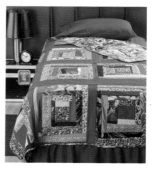
32 Crazy Blocks Quilt

40 Raggedy Log Cabin

48 Desert Sun Pillow

57 Pineapple Four-Patch

64 Every Which Way

71 Lights in the Cabin

74 Autumn Hues Quarter Blocks

77 Triangle Beginnings

80 Basket of Flowers

84 Rose Cabin Coasters

87 Carved in Stone Place Mat

92 Wrapped in Roses

95 Log Cabin Slouchy Bag

100 Orange Blossoms at the Cabin

107 Oversized Quilt Carryall

112 Lacy Bible Cover

120 Who's At the Zoo?

123 Blissful in the Clouds

128 Lots of Dots Baby Blocks

132 Stripes & Dots Baby Bib

135 Peppermint Candy Christmas

140 Cabins of Democracy

144 Apple of My Eye

148 Pumpkin Patch Table Runner

152 On the Town Square

157 Double Lightning

160 Windfall

166 Mod Quads

170 Go Green Table Topper

SPECIAL THANKS

Please join us in thanking the talented designers below.

Arlene Bauman
160, Windfall

Karen Blocher
6, Piecing With Strips

Barbara Clayton
112, Lacy Bible Cover
135, Peppermint Candy Christmas

Brenda Connelly/Barbara Miller
9, Crack in the Wall

Phyllis Dobbs
77, Triangle Beginnings

Gina Gempesaw
157, Double Lightning
166, Mod Quads

Bev Getschel
152, On the Town Square

Sandra L. Hatch
52, Paper Piecing From the Top
57, Pineapple Four-Patch

Julie Higgins
24, Free-Form Foundation Piecing
27, La Luz Del Sol

Connie Kauffman
14, Paper Piecing
18, Radiant Star
87, Carved in Stone Place Mat
92, Wrapped in Roses

Chris Malone
80, Basket of Flowers
84, Rose Cabin Coasters
107, Oversized Quilt Carryall
120, Who's at the Zoo?

Merry May
36, Easy Ragged Edge
40, Raggedy Log Cabin

Connie Rand
170, Go Green Table Topper

Judith Sandstrom
71, Lights in the Cabin

Wendy Sheppard
74, Autumn Hues Quarter Blocks
123, Blissful in the Clouds
144, Apple of My Eye
148, Pumpkin Patch Table Runner

Stephanie Smith
44, Folding & Pleating Strips
48, Desert Sun Pillow

Norma Storm
64, Every Which Way

Carolyn S. Vagts
100, Orange Blossoms at the Cabin

Julie Weaver
140, Cabins of Democracy

Carol Zentgraf
30, Quilt As You Go
32, Crazy Blocks Quilt
95, Log Cabin Slouchy Bag
128, Lots of Dots Baby Blocks
132, Stripes & Dots Baby Bib

FABRIC & SUPPLIES

Page 18: Radiant Star—PolyLite® thread from Sulky™ Inc.

Page 32: Crazy Blocks Quilt—April Showers Bring Sunflowers fabric collection from Free Spirit's Art of Possibilities Studios for Westminster Fabrics; Cotton Classic batting from Fairfield Processing Corp.; Steam-A-Seam 2 fusible web tape from The Warm Company.

Page 44: Folded Log Cabin Technique—Garden Party fabric collection from Moda.

Page 57: Pineapple Four Patch—Tuscany bleached cotton batting from Hobbs Bonded Fiber and Star Quilting Thread from Coats.

Page 64: Every Which Way—Professionally machine-quilted by Pam Higgins of Huggs'n Quilts.

Page 74: Autumn Hues Quarter Blocks—Summer Solstice, Everything but the Kitchen Sink, Crazy for Dots and Stripes, Pindots and Jinny Beyer Palette fabric collections from RJR; Mako 50 cotton thread from Aurifil; Tuscany Silk Batt from Hobbs Bonded Fiber.

Page 77: Triangle Beginnings—Couleur Vie fabric collection by Brenda Pinnick for Henry Glass & Co. Purple fabric from Quilting Treasures; cotton batting from The Warm Company; Blendables multicolored thread from Sulky of America; all-purpose thread from Coats.

Page 87: Carved in Stone Place Mat—Stonehenge/Colorado Fabrics from Northcott Silk; Warm and Natural cotton batting from The Warm Company; PolyLite™ Thread from Sulky of America.

Page 95: Log Cabin Slouchy Bag—Mon Sheri fabric collection from Robert Kaufman; Cotton Classic batting from Fairfield Processing Corp.

Page 100: Orange Blossoms at the Cabin—No. 345 fusible web and No. 395 Katahdin Autumn batting from Bosal Foam, Fiber, Interfacing and Crafts.

Page 120: Who's at the Zoo?—Hooty Hoot Kangaroo fabric collection for Doohickey Designs by Riley Blake Designs.

Page 123: Blissful in the Clouds—Mako 50 cotton thread from Aurifil; Tuscany Silk batting from Hobbs Bonded Fiber; Flower Power, Handspray and Shasta fabric collection from RJR Fabrics.

Page 128: Lots of Dots Baby Blocks—Remix fabric collection from Robert Kaufman; Poly-fil fiberfill from Fairfield Processing Corp; SteamASeam 2 fusible web sheets from The Warm Company.

Page 132: Stripes & Dots Baby Bib—Remix fabric collection from Robert Kaufman; SteamASeam 2 fusible web from The Warm Company.

Page 140: Cabins of Democracy—Thermore(R) Ultra-thin batting from Hobbs Bonded Fiber.

Page 144: Apple of My Eye—Everything But the Kitchen Sink, Crazy for Dots and Stripes, Jinny Beyer Palette and Pindot fabric collections from RJR Fabrics; Tuscany Silk Batting from Hobbs Bonded Fiber; Mako 50 cotton thread from Aurifil.

Page 148: Pumpkin Patch Table Runner—Everything But the Kitchen Sink, Crazy for Dots and Stripes, Jinny Beyer Palette and Pindot fabric collections from RJR Fabrics; Tuscany Silk Batting from Hobbs Bonded Fiber; Mako 50 cotton thread from Aurifil.

Page 152: On the Town Square—Luna Notte fabric collection by 3 Sisters for Moda; Nature-fill Bamboo batting from Fairfield Processing.

Page 170: Go Green Table Topper—Star Machine Quilting thread from Coats.